ARGOPREP

TEACHER RECOMMENDED

8th GRADE
COMMON CORE
MATH

DAILY PRACTICE BOOK

ARGOPREP.COM

FREE ONLINE SYSTEM WITH VIDEO EXPLANATIONS

ArgoPrep is one of the leading providers of supplemental educational products and services. We offer affordable and effective test prep solutions to educators, parents and students. Learning should be fun and easy! For that reason, most of our workbooks come with detailed video answer explanations taught by one of our fabulous instructors.

Our goal is to make your life easier, so let us know how we can help you by e-mailing us at: info@argoprep.com.

ALL RIGHTS RESERVED
Copyright © 2022 by Argo Brothers, Inc.

ISBN: 9781951048945

Published by Argo Brothers, Inc.

All rights reserved, no part of this book may be reproduced or distributed in any form or by any means without the written permission of Argo Brothers, Inc.

All the materials within are the exclusive property of Argo Brothers, Inc.

ArgoPrep has won **over 10+ educational awards** for their workbooks and online learning platform. Here are a few highlighted awards!

TABLE OF CONTENTS

Week 1 - *Rational & Irrational Numbers* 11
Week 2 - *Approximating Rational & Irrational Numbers* 17
Week 3 - *Properties of Exponents* 23
Week 4 - *Square Roots & Cube Roots* 29
Week 5 - *Scientific Notation* 35
Week 6 - *Slope, Distance, and Coordinate graphs* 41
Week 7 - *Working with Linear Equations* 46
Week 8 - *Functions, Inputs, Outputs and Analysis of graphs* 53
Week 9 - *Functions continued* 59
Week 10 - *Linear vs. Nonlinear Functions* 65
Week 11 - *Rotations, Reflections, and Translations* 71
Week 12 - *Types of Transformations* 77
Week 13 - *Understanding angle rules when parallel lines are cut by a transversal* 83
Week 14 - *Pythagorean Theorem* 89
Week 15 - *Finding distance using Pythagorean Theorem* 95
Week 16 - *Finding volume for cones, cylinders, and spheres* 101
Week 17 - *Scatter Plots* 107
Week 18 - *Best Fit of Line* 113
Week 19 - *Understanding equations of a linear model* 119
Week 20 - *Table, Charts and Analyzing Data* 125
End of Year Assessment 133
Answer Key 143

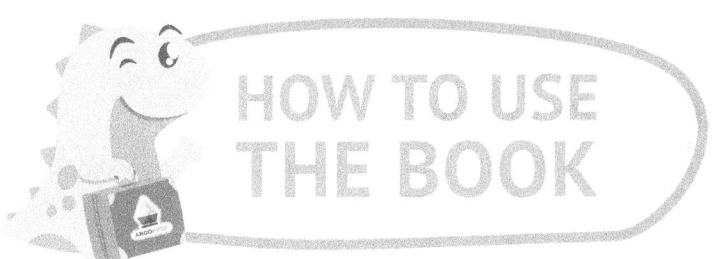

HOW TO USE THE BOOK

This workbook is designed to give lots of practice with the math Common Core State Standards (CCSS). By practicing and mastering this entire workbook, your child will become very familiar and comfortable with the state math exam. If you are a teacher using this workbook for your students, you will notice each question is labeled with the specific standard so you can easily assign your students problems in the workbook. This workbook takes the CCSS and divides them up among 20 weeks. By working on these problems on a daily basis, students will be able to (1) find any deficiencies in their understanding and/or practice of math and (2) have small successes each day that will build proficiency and confidence in their abilities.

We strongly recommend watching the videos, as they will reinforce the fundamental concepts. Please note, scrap paper may be necessary while using this workbook so that the student has sufficient space to show their work.

For a detailed overview of the Common Core State Standards for 8th grade, please visit: www.corestandards.org/Math/Content/8/introduction/

HOW TO WATCH VIDEO EXPLANATIONS
IT IS ABSOLUTELY FREE

Go to **argoprep.com/ccm8**
OR scan the QR Code:

OTHER BOOKS BY ARGOPREP

Here are some other test prep workbooks by ArgoPrep you may be interested in. All of our workbooks come equipped with detailed video explanations to make your learning experience a breeze! Visit us at *www.argoprep.com*

COMMON CORE MATH SERIES

COMMON CORE ELA SERIES

INTRODUCING MATH!

Introducing Math! by ArgoPrep is an award-winning series created by certified teachers to provide students with high-quality practice problems. Our workbooks include topic overviews with instruction, practice questions, answer explanations along with digital access to video explanations. Practice in confidence - with ArgoPrep!

SCIENCE SERIES

Science Daily Practice Workbook by ArgoPrep is an award-winning series created by certified science teachers to help build mastery of foundational science skills. Our workbooks explore science topics in depth with ArgoPrep's 5 E'S to build science mastery.

KIDS SUMMER ACADEMY SERIES

ArgoPrep's Kids Summer Academy series helps prevent summer learning loss and gets students ready for their new school year by reinforcing core foundations in math, english and science. Our workbooks also introduce new concepts so students can get a head start and be on top of their game for the new school year!

CAPTAIN BRAVERY

WATER FIRE

MYSTICAL NINJA

GREEN POISON

FIRESTORM WARRIOR

RAPID NINJA

CAPTAIN ARGO

THUNDER WARRIOR

ADRASTOS THE SUPER WARRIOR

DANCE HERO

GREEN DRAGON WARRIOR

WEEK 1

Week 1 is all about working with rational and irrational numbers.

**You can find detailed video explanations of each problem in the book by visiting:
ArgoPrep.com/ccm8**

WEEK 1 : DAY 1

1. Which of the following numbers is irrational?

   A. $6.\overline{77}$
   B. 7.763892...
   C. 34.26
   D. 16,785

   8.NS.A.1

2. Which of the following numbers is rational?

   A. $\sqrt{16}$
   B. $\sqrt{8}$
   C. 56.0712...
   D. π

   8.NS.A.1

3. Which of the following numbers is NOT rational?

   A. $\frac{42}{56}$
   B. 3.045045...
   C. $\sqrt{25}$
   D. $2\sqrt{19}$

   8.NS.A.1

4. Choose an option which contains ONLY rational numbers?

   A. $65.888...; \sqrt{42}; \frac{702}{31}; 2\pi$
   B. $97; 3\sqrt{25}; -\frac{13}{12}; 26,789$
   C. $\frac{68}{3}; 2.07239...; \sqrt{2}; -27$
   D. $9.207; -\frac{\sqrt{16}}{2}; 5\pi; -\frac{1}{23}$

   8.NS.A.1

5. Is the number $0.\overline{6}$ rational or irrational?

   Answer: _____

   8.NS.A.1

6. Convert the number $\frac{\sqrt{16}}{5}$ into a decimal. Is it a rational number?

   Answer: _____

   8.NS.A.1

An irrational number is a real number that cannot be written as a simple fraction.

12

WEEK 1 : DAY 2

1. Which fraction is the same as the rational number 2.666667?

   A. $\dfrac{8}{3}$ C. $\dfrac{12}{5}$

   B. $\dfrac{6}{4}$ D. $\dfrac{14}{8}$

   8.NS.A.1

2. Which of the following numbers is irrational?

   A. $-\dfrac{6}{16}$ C. $\dfrac{\sqrt{8}}{2}$

   B. 7.0398   D. 6,907

   8.NS.A.1

3. Which of the following numbers is rational?

   A. $\sqrt{121}$ C. $\sqrt{122}$

   B. $\sqrt{68}$ D. $\sqrt{72}$

   8.NS.A.1

4. Which fraction is the same as the irrational number 1.41421356...?

   A. $\dfrac{15}{7}$ C. $\dfrac{\sqrt{4}}{2}$

   B. $\dfrac{\sqrt{8}}{2}$ D. $\dfrac{\sqrt{9}}{4}$

   8.NS.A.1

5. Convert the decimal 0.375 into a simple fraction. Is this number rational or irrational?

   Answer: _____

   8.NS.A.1

6. Is the number $\dfrac{\sqrt{25}}{\sqrt{16}}$ rational or irrational?

   Answer: _____

   8.NS.A.1

TIP of the DAY

π is an irrational number that has no pattern and has over a quadrillion decimal places.

13

WEEK 1 : DAY 3

1. Which choice contains ONLY irrational numbers?

   A. $-7.652;\ \sqrt{14}\ ;\ 6.932781...;\ \dfrac{2\pi}{3}$

   B. $2\sqrt{64};\ 5.7562347...;\ \sqrt{6};\ -\dfrac{1}{50}$

   C. $\dfrac{3}{\sqrt{7}}\ ;\ 7.6438913...;\ 9\sqrt{45};\ 4\pi$

   D. $-\dfrac{43}{12};\ \dfrac{1}{\sqrt{4}};\ 5.7\overline{689}...;\ -10.034$

   8.NS.A.1

2. Which number should be put into the blank to get an irrational number?

   $5.678 +$ _____

   A. $8.7676...$ C. -65

   B. $\sqrt{8}$ D. $\dfrac{3}{5}$

   8.NS.A.1

3. Convert the number $0.\overline{88}$ into a simple fraction.

   Answer: _____

   8.NS.A.1

4. Which of the following numbers is rational?

   A. $\sqrt{65}$

   B. $\sqrt{64}$

   C. $-\sqrt{82}$

   D. $\sqrt{40}$

   8.NS.A.1

5. Mr. Hopkins asked his students to calculate the result of $50 + 20\left(\sqrt{32} + 7\right)$. Is the result of the calculations a rational or an irrational number?

   Answer: _____

   8.NS.A.1

6. Which rational number is NOT equal to the number $\dfrac{5\sqrt{9}}{45}$?

   A. $\dfrac{1}{3}$ C. $\dfrac{15 \times 3}{45}$

   B. $0.333...$ D. $\dfrac{76}{228}$

   8.NS.A.1

TIP of the DAY

If we multiply two irrational numbers, will the result always be irrational? Not always!
$\sqrt{2} \times \sqrt{2} = 2$
As you can see, multiplying irrational numbers may also result in a rational number.

14

WEEK 1 : DAY 4

1. Which of the following numbers is irrational?

   A. $\sqrt{625}$

   B. $-\dfrac{\sqrt{26}}{4}$

   C. $-\dfrac{5}{\sqrt{121}}$

   D. 3.27^2

   8.NS.A.1

2. Which simple fraction equals the number $1.0\overline{6}$?

   A. $\dfrac{16}{14}$

   B. $\dfrac{8}{3}$

   C. $\dfrac{16}{15}$

   D. $\dfrac{4}{3}$

   8.NS.A.1

3. Is the number $5\sqrt{50}$ rational or irrational?

   Answer: _____

   8.NS.A.1

4. Write an irrational number on the line below.

   Answer: _____

   8.NS.A.1

5. Which number should be put into the blank to get a rational number?

   _____ - 45.086

   A. $3\sqrt{5}$

   B. $\sqrt{144}$

   C. 56.97834...

   D. 48π

   8.NS.A.1

5. If you take a whole number and multiply it by $\sqrt{7}$, you will get a:

   A. Whole number
   B. Rational number
   C. Irrational number
   D. Natural number

   8.NS.A.1

Rational numbers are any numbers that can be expressed as a ratio or a simple fraction.

WEEK 1 : DAY 5

ASSESSMENT

1. Which fraction corresponds to the number $5.\overline{07}$?

   A. $5\frac{7}{9}$ C. $5\frac{70}{90}$

   B. $5\frac{7}{90}$ D. $5\frac{7}{99}$

   8.NS.A.1

2. Which of the following numbers is rational?

   A. 6.0760789...
   B. $\sqrt{225}$
   C. 6π
   D. $4\sqrt{12}$

   8.NS.A.1

3. Which expression results in a rational number?

   A. $2\sqrt{9} + 3\sqrt{16}$ C. $\frac{7}{8} \times \sqrt{6}$

   B. $3\sqrt{3} + 5\sqrt{5}$ D. $\frac{\pi}{8} - \sqrt{122}$

   8.NS.A.1

4. Which number is NOT irrational?

   A. $-\frac{10}{\sqrt{2}}$ C. $\sqrt{45} + \sqrt{45}$

   B. $-\frac{54}{54}$ D. π^2

   8.NS.A.1

5. Is the number $\dfrac{(6.\overline{765} + 7.\overline{235})}{\sqrt{36}}$ rational or irrational?

   Answer: _____

   8.NS.A.1

6. Which of the following numbers is NOT rational?

   A. $6\sqrt{144}$ C. $-\frac{44}{44}$

   B. $\frac{65}{\sqrt{88}}$ D. $\frac{6\pi}{\pi}$

   8.NS.A.1

DAY 6
Challenge question

Is the result of this expression $\dfrac{5\pi}{3\pi} + 4.\overline{389}$ a rational or irrational number?

Answer: _____

8.NS.A.1

16

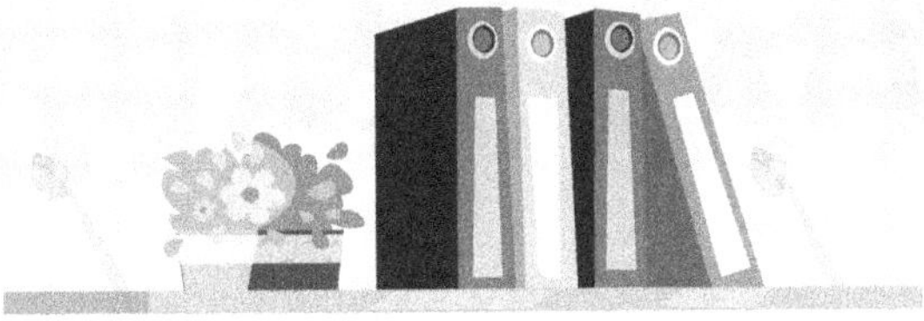

WEEK 2

ARGOPREP.COM

VIDEO
EXPLANATIONS

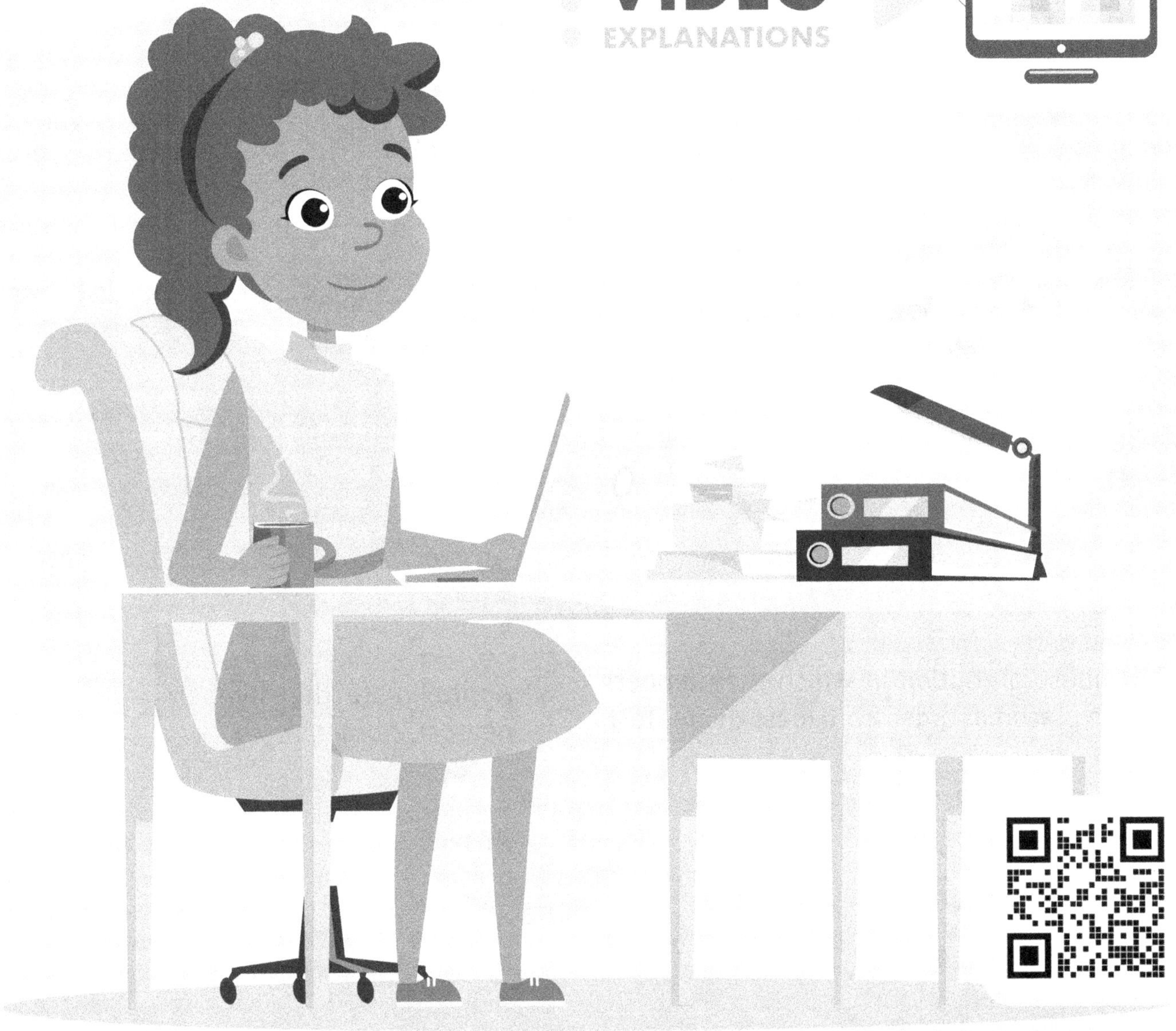

In week 2 we will be approximating irrational numbers and locating irrational numbers on a number line.

You can find detailed video explanations of each problem in the book by visiting: ArgoPrep.com/ccm8

WEEK 2 : DAY 1

1. $\sqrt{20}$ is between what two integers?

   A. 1 and 2
   B. 3 and 4
   C. 4 and 5
   D. 5 and 6

   8.NS.A.2

2. Which number is greater than $\sqrt{70}$?

   A. 6
   B. 7
   C. 8
   D. 9

   8.NS.A.2

3. Choose an option in which the numbers are placed in order from least to greatest.

   A. $\sqrt{46}; 3\sqrt{25}; 4\sqrt{18}$
   B. $4\sqrt{9}; \sqrt{56}; 5\sqrt{12}$
   C. $3.2; \sqrt{15}; \sqrt{6}$
   D. $2\sqrt{47}; 3\pi; 4\frac{7}{8}$

   8.NS.A.2

4. Which expression is true?

   A. $3\sqrt{15} > 2\sqrt{129}$
   B. $4\sqrt{15} < 7\sqrt{5}$
   C. $6\sqrt{28} < 5\sqrt{38}$
   D. $\sqrt{52} > 7.86$

   8.NS.A.2

5. Place the numbers below in order from least to greatest

   $4\sqrt{32};\quad 26;\quad 5\sqrt{17};\quad \frac{\sqrt{68}}{2}.$

   Answer: _____

   8.NS.A.2

6. Approximate the number $\sqrt{57}$ to the nearest integer.

   Answer: _____

   8.NS.A.2

TIP of the DAY

A quick way to determine if a number is irrational is writing the number in decimal form. If there is no pattern and the decimal goes on forever, the number is irrational.

18

WEEK 2 : DAY 2

1. Which number is less than $4\sqrt{43}$?

   A. 32
   B. 25
   C. 29
   D. 35

2. Which number should be put in the blank to make this statement true?

   $$9.327 > \underline{\qquad}$$

   A. $\sqrt{82}$ C. $3\sqrt{75}$
   B. $2\sqrt{42}$ D. $2\sqrt{38}$

3. $\sqrt{64}$ can be represented where on the number line below?

   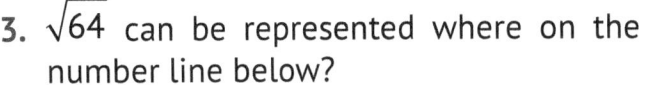

   A. 6   C. 8
   B. 7   D. 9

4. What is $\sqrt{39}$ approximated to the hundredths place?

   A. 6.38
   B. 6.99
   C. 6.32
   D. 6.24

5. Use rational approximation to place the number $\sqrt{44}$ on the given number line.

   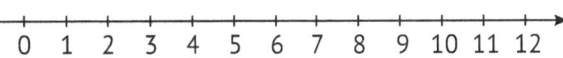

6. Place the numbers below in order from greatest to least.

   $$\sqrt{74};\quad 2\sqrt{32};\quad \frac{\sqrt{85}}{3};\quad 9\frac{25}{40}$$

   Answer: _____

TIP of the DAY

Can negative numbers be rational? Of course! As long as the number can be expressed as a simple fraction, it is a rational number.

WEEK 2 : DAY 3

1. $2\sqrt{41}$ is between what two integers?

   A. 11 and 12
   B. 12 and 13
   C. 13 and 14
   D. 14 and 15

2. Which number is equal to $5\sqrt{74}$?

   A. 42.99
   B. 43.87
   C. 44.02
   D. 43.01

3. Which of the following numbers is the greatest in value?

   $\sqrt{65}$; $9\frac{6}{7}$; $3\sqrt[3]{24}$; $2\sqrt{15}$

   Answer: _____

4. Which number should be put in the blank to complete the following inequality?

   $5 < \underline{\qquad} < 6$

   A. $2\sqrt{15}$ C. $4\sqrt{3}$
   B. $3\sqrt{2}$ D. $\frac{\sqrt{120}}{2}$

5. Without using a calculator, put the irrational numbers on the number line.

   $\frac{\sqrt{48}}{2}$; $2\sqrt{26}$; $2\frac{\sqrt{2}}{4}$

   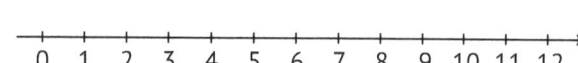

6. Which irrational number is greater than 28?

   A. $3\sqrt{76}$
   B. $5\sqrt{33}$
   C. $\sqrt{154}$
   D. $6\sqrt{17}$

TIP of the DAY

In this week, we are placing irrational numbers on a number line. In order to do this easily, simply determine between what two integers this irrational number lies on.

WEEK 2 : DAY 4

1. Without using a calculator, match each expression to the correct point and fill in the blanks given below.

   $\sqrt{21}$ -2π $-2\sqrt{14}$ $\sqrt{5}$

   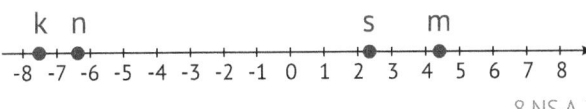

2. Which of the following comparison statements is true?

   A. $4\sqrt{20} > 3\sqrt{50}$
   B. $\dfrac{\sqrt{13}}{2} > \dfrac{\sqrt{23}}{3}$
   C. $\sqrt{46} < 6.3\overline{59}$
   D. $\sqrt{64} < \sqrt{24}$

3. $-5\sqrt{85}$ is between what two integers?

   A. 34 and 35
   B. -32 and -33
   C. -15 and 15
   D. -46 and -47

4. Approximate $3 \times \sqrt[3]{27} \times \pi$ to the nearest integer.

   A. 25
   B. 28
   C. 33
   D. 36

5. Fill in the blank with a comparison symbol

   $7\sqrt{28}$ _____ $6\sqrt{30}$

   Answer: _____

6. Which number corresponds to point k in the given drawing?

   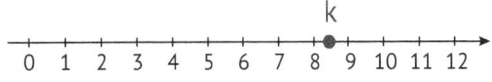

   A. $\sqrt{70}$ C. $2\sqrt{30}$
   B. $\sqrt{75}$ D. $3\sqrt{20}$

TIP of the DAY

When you compare two irrational numbers, use approximation to quickly determine which of the two irrational numbers is greater.

WEEK 2 : DAY 5

ASSESSMENT

1. $-2\sqrt{37}$ is approximated to which of the following integers?

   A. -11
   B. -12
   C. -13
   D. 13

   8.NS.A.2

2. Which of the following irrational numbers is the least in value?

   A. $\sqrt{5}$
   B. $-\sqrt{42}$
   C. $-2\sqrt{23}$
   D. -3π

   8.NS.A.2

3. Without using a calculator, fill in the blanks with two consecutive integers to complete the following inequality.

   _____ < $\sqrt{67}$ < _____

   8.NS.A.2

4. Without using a calculator, plot the following irrational numbers on the number line.

   $\sqrt{31}$; $2\sqrt{10}$; $-\sqrt{17}$; $-\sqrt{8}$

   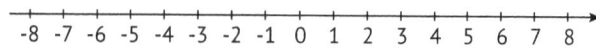

   8.NS.A.2

5. Which comparison statement is FALSE?

   A. $\sqrt{145} < 12\sqrt{3}$
   B. $-5\sqrt{14} > -3\sqrt{21}$
   C. $\dfrac{4\sqrt{8}}{3} > \dfrac{5\sqrt{7}}{6}$
   D. $2\sqrt{2} < \sqrt{39}$

   8.NS.A.2

6. $\sqrt{33}$ is approximated to which of the following integers?

   A. 4
   B. 5
   C. 6
   D. 7

   8.NS.A.2

DAY 6
Challenge question

Fill in the blank with a comparison symbol.

$\dfrac{5}{\sqrt{44}}$ _____ $\dfrac{4}{\sqrt{35}}$

8.NS.A.2

22

WEEK 3

ARGOPREP.COM

VIDEO
EXPLANATIONS

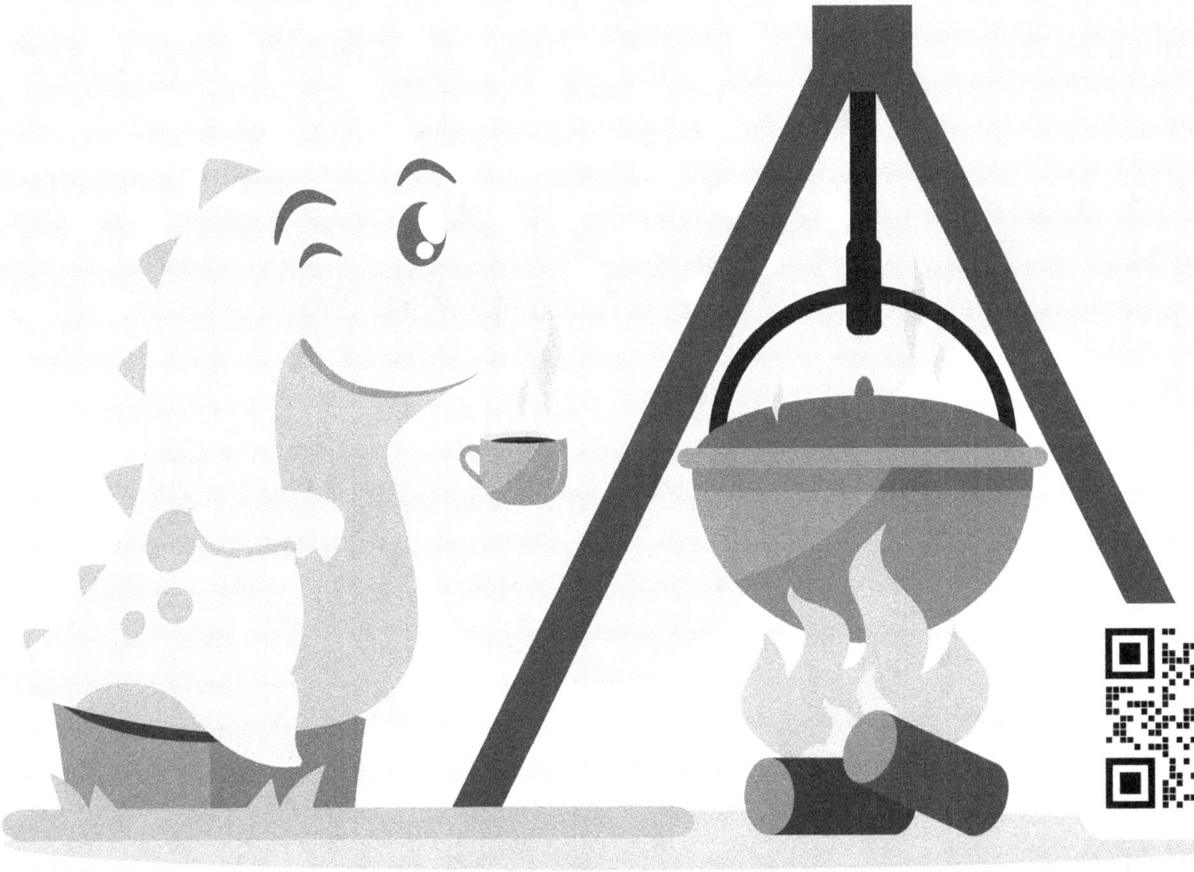

Week 3 is all about the properties of exponents and finding equivalent numerical expressions.

You can find detailed video explanations of each problem in the book by visiting:
ArgoPrep.com/ccm8

WEEK 3 : DAY 1

1. Select the equivalent expression of x^5.

    A. $x^3 + x^2$
    B. $x^3 \times x^2$
    C. $(x^3)^2$
    D. $x^3 \div x^2$

    8.EE.A.1

2. What is $x^4 \times y^4$?

    A. $(x \times y)^8$
    B. $x \times y^8$
    C. $x \times y^{16}$
    D. $(x \times y)^4$

    8.EE.A.1

3. What is $(x \times x \times x \times x \times x \times x)(y \times y \times y \times y \times y \times y \times y)$?

    A. xy^{12}
    B. $(xy)^{12}$
    C. $x^5 y^7$
    D. $(xy)^{35}$

    8.EE.A.1

4. Simplify the expression: $(4x^7)^2$

    Answer: _____

    8.EE.A.1

5. Select the equivalent expression of $27x^{18}$

    A. $(3x^6)^3$
    B. $(3^3 x^6)^3$
    C. $(3^3 x^3)^3$
    D. $3x^{18}$

    8.EE.A.1

6. What is n in the expression:

    $(8^3 \times 9^4)^2 = 8^n \times 9^8$

    Answer: _____

    8.EE.A.1

Fun Fact: Any number raised to the 0 power is 1.
$5^0 = 1$

WEEK 3 : DAY 2

1. Select the equivalent expression of $16x^8$
   A. $(16x^6)^2$
   B. $16x^4 + x^8$
   C. $(8x^4)^2$
   D. $(2^4 x^3) \times x^5$

   8.EE.A.1

2. What is $4x^6 \div 2x^2$?
   A. $4x^8$
   B. $4x^3$
   C. $2x^4$
   D. $2x^8$

   8.EE.A.1

3. What is the value of n in the expression:
   $$\frac{2^2 \times 4^8}{4^4} = 4^n?$$
   A. 4
   B. 5
   C. 8
   D. 12

   8.EE.A.1

4. Christian solved the following expression: $\frac{2x^2}{2x} \times \frac{2x^4}{x^2}$. He found four different solutions. One of them is FALSE. Find the solution that is not true.

   A. $2x^5$
   B. $\frac{(2x^3)^2}{2x^3}$
   C. $\frac{4x^6}{2x^3}$
   D. $2x^3$

   8.EE.A.1

5. Write the expression $\frac{(4x^5)^2}{8x^{12}}$ in the form bx^n.

   Answer: _____

   8.EE.A.1

6. Write the expression $x^2 \times \frac{8x^2}{x} + 4x^3$ in the form bx^n.

   Answer: _____

   8.EE.A.1

TIP of the DAY

When you multiply two exponents that have the same base, keep the base the same and add the two exponents.
$x^4 \times x^5 = x^9$

WEEK 3 : DAY 3

1. Select the equivalent expression of $2x^{-4}$.

   A. $6x^{-6} - 4x^2$

   B. $\dfrac{6x}{3x^5}$

   C. $(2x^5)^{-20}$

   D. $\dfrac{2x}{2x^{-5}}$

2. What is the value of k and n in the expression: $\dfrac{(x^2y^3)^4}{x^3y^{15}} = x^k y^n$?

   A. $k = 6; n = 4$
   C. $k = 5; n = -3$

   B. $k = 5; n = 3$
   D. $k = -5; n = 4$

3. Which expression gives $\dfrac{2}{x^3}$?

   A. $2x^2 \dfrac{1}{x^4}$
   C. $2x^{-2} \dfrac{1}{x^{-5}}$

   B. $2x^{-2} \dfrac{1}{x}$
   D. $2x^2 \times x^{-4}$

4. Which expression is NOT equivalent to $\left(\dfrac{4x^2}{8y^5}\right)^2$?

   A. $\dfrac{4x^4}{8y^{10}}$
   C. $\dfrac{1}{4}x^4 y^{-10}$

   B. $\dfrac{16x^4}{64y^{10}}$
   D. $\dfrac{x^4}{4y^{10}}$

5. Write the expression $4x^6 \times y^{-10} \times x^2$ in the form $\left(\dfrac{ax}{by}\right)^n$.

   Answer: _____

6. What is the value of k and n in the expression: $\dfrac{10x^4}{15y^7} \times \left(\dfrac{x}{y}\right)^3 = \dfrac{2}{3} x^k y^n$?

   Answer: _____

TIP of the DAY

When you divide two exponents that have the same base, keep the base the same and subtract the two exponents. $\dfrac{x^5}{x^3} = x^2$

WEEK 3 : DAY 4

1. What is $(6x)^2 \div 4x^5$?

   A. $6x \div 4^{-3}$

   B. $\dfrac{2}{3}x^{-3}$

   C. $\dfrac{9}{x^3}$

   D. $\dfrac{6}{4}x^{-3}$

   8.EE.A.1

2. Which expression is NOT equivalent to $2^{12}x^{10}$?

   A. $\dfrac{(2^2 x^2)^7}{4x^4}$

   B. $\dfrac{2^{14}x^{14}}{4x^4}$

   C. $\dfrac{2^{14}}{4}x^{14}x^{-4}$

   D. $2^{14}x^{14} \div 4x^{-4}$

   8.EE.A.1

3. What is $\left(\dfrac{2x^3}{8x^4}\right)^3$?

   A. $\dfrac{1x^6}{4x^7}$

   B. $\dfrac{1}{64x^3}$

   C. $\dfrac{2x^3}{64x^4}$

   D. $\dfrac{1x^9}{4x^{12}}$

   8.EE.A.1

4. Write the expression $2(x^2 \div x^{-4})^5$ in the form bx^n.

   Answer: _____

   8.EE.A.1

5. What is $\left(\dfrac{3x^4}{6x^7}\right)^{-2}$?

   A. $4x^6$

   B. $\dfrac{3x^{14}}{x^8}$

   C. $\dfrac{6x^{-8}}{3x^{-14}}$

   D. $3x^6$

   8.EE.A.1

6. Find the value of n in the equation:

   $$\dfrac{9x^{10}}{16y^{12}} = \left(\dfrac{4y^6}{3x^5}\right)^n$$

   Answer: _____

   8.EE.A.1

TIP of the DAY

Make sure you know the negative exponent rule. If you have a negative exponent in the numerator, you can move the exponent to the denominator and the exponent will be positive. For example: $a^{-n} = \dfrac{1}{a^n}$

WEEK 3 : DAY 5

ASSESSMENT

1. What is $(8x^{-2})^3$?

   A. $8x^{-6}$

   B. $24x^{-6}$

   C. $\dfrac{8 \times 3}{x^6}$

   D. $\dfrac{8^3}{x^6}$

4. Simplify the expression $\dfrac{(2x^2)^4}{8x^{15}}$.

   Answer: _____

2. Select the equivalent expression for $\left(\dfrac{2^3 x^2}{5y^4}\right)^{-3}$.

   A. $\dfrac{2^6 x^{-6}}{5y^{-12}}$

   B. $\dfrac{5^3 y^{12}}{8^3 x^6}$

   C. $\dfrac{2^6 x^{-6}}{5^3 y^{-12}}$

   D. $\dfrac{2^3 x^{-6}}{5y^{-12}}$

5. What is $\dfrac{2x^{-3}}{4x^5} \times x^4$?

   A. $\dfrac{1}{2x^4}$

   B. $\dfrac{2}{x^8}$

   C. x^{-17}

   D. $\dfrac{2}{x^{17}}$

3. What is the value of n in the equation $\left(\dfrac{5x^2 y^3}{x^4}\right)^n = 1$?

   A. 3

   B. 5

   C. 0

   D. 2

6. Solve the following equation:

   $$\left(\dfrac{4^4}{4^3}\right)^{-2} = \dfrac{4^{12}}{x^{14}}$$

   Answer: _____

DAY 6
Challenge question

Rewrite the expression $\left(\dfrac{x^{-8}}{y^{-4}}\right)^3$ in the form $\dfrac{x^n}{y^k}$.

_____

28

WEEK 4

VIDEO EXPLANATIONS

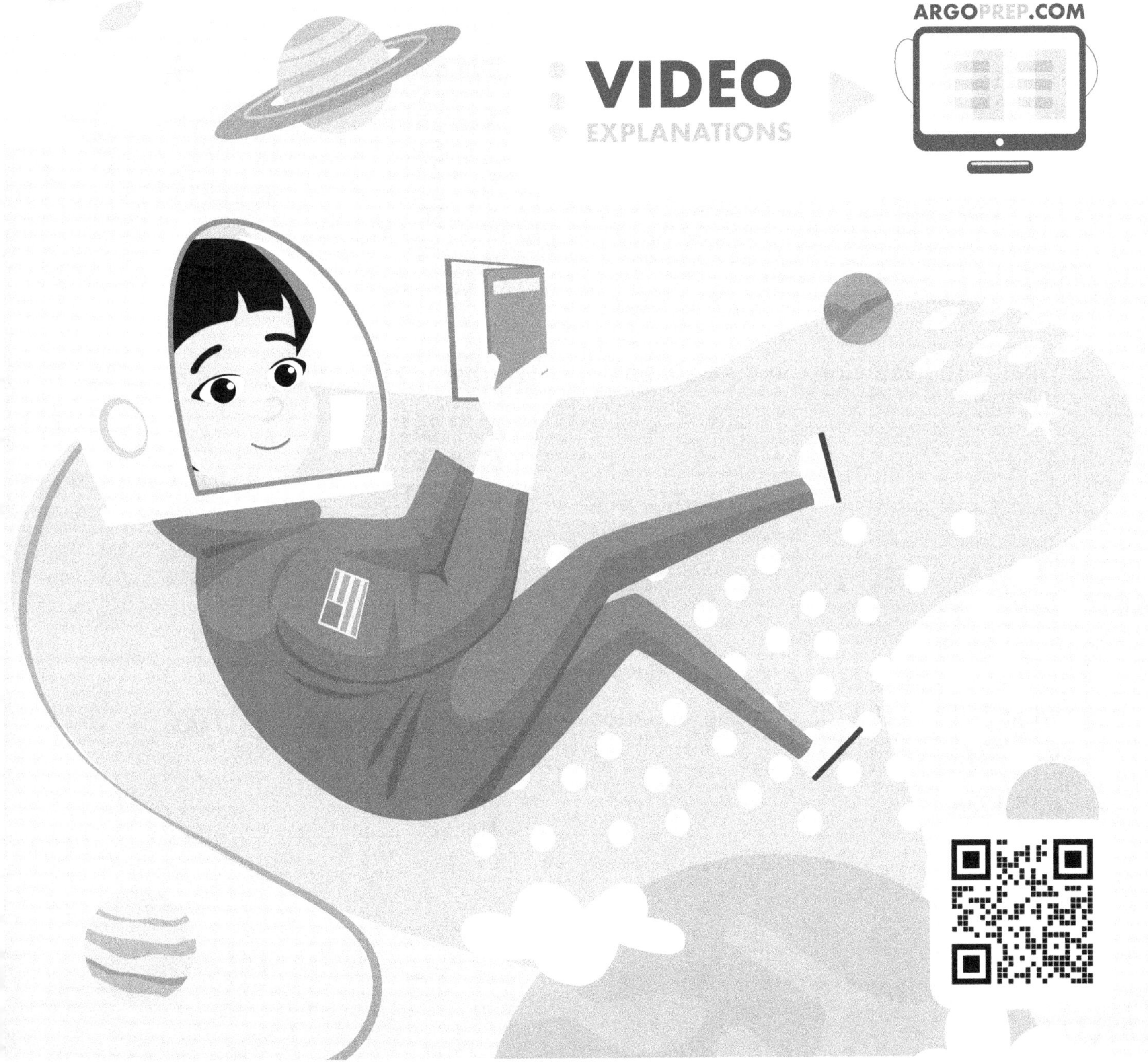

In week 4 we will work with problems dealing with square roots and cube roots.

You can find detailed video explanations of each problem in the book by visiting: ArgoPrep.com/ccm8

WEEK 4 : DAY 1

1. What is 15^2?

   A. 215
   B. 225
   C. 235
   D. 245

2. What is the value of x in the equation $\sqrt{x} = 3$?

   A. 27
   B. 26
   C. 9
   D. 3

3. What is the value of x in the equation $\sqrt[3]{x} = 8$?

   A. 512
   B. 482
   C. 532
   D. 601

4. Which square root results in a rational number?

   A. $\sqrt{15}$
   B. $\sqrt{25}$
   C. $\sqrt{30}$
   D. $\sqrt{17}$

5. What is 21^3?

   A. 9,261
   B. 8,761
   C. 7,931
   D. 9,981

6. What is the solution of $\sqrt{36}$?

   Answer: _____

An exponent only applies to what is immediately in front of it. $(-3)^2 = (-3)(-3) = +9$ but $-3^2 = -(3)(3) = -9$.

WEEK 4 : DAY 2

1. What is 36^2?

   A. 1,296
   B. 1,136
   C. 1,256
   D. 1,346

2. What is the value of x in the equation $\sqrt{x} = 15$?

   A. 215
   B. 225
   C. 235
   D. 245

3. What is the value of x in the equation $\sqrt[3]{x} = 6$?

   A. 64
   B. 78
   C. 216
   D. 236

4. Which square root results in a rational number?

   A. $\sqrt{225}$
   B. $\sqrt{112}$
   C. $\sqrt{89}$
   D. $\sqrt{68}$

5. Which of the following results in an irrational number?

   A. $\sqrt[3]{8}$
   B. $\sqrt{89}$
   C. $\sqrt[3]{27}$
   D. $\sqrt{49}$

6. What is the value of $\sqrt[3]{125}$?

   Answer: _____

TIP of the DAY

If you have time, be sure to double check your calculations to avoid common calculation errors.

WEEK 4 : DAY 3

1. What is 12^3?

   A. 1,458
   B. 1,328
   C. 1,728
   D. 1,638

2. What is the value of x in the equation $\sqrt{x} = 34$?

   A. 1,246
   B. 1,356
   C. 1,276
   D. 1,156

3. What is the value of x in the equation $\sqrt[3]{x} = 12$?

   A. 1,548
   B. 1,378
   C. 1,428
   D. 1,728

4. Which of the following results in a rational number?

   A. $\sqrt[3]{89}$
   B. $\sqrt[3]{136}$
   C. $\sqrt[3]{64}$
   D. $\sqrt[3]{124}$

5. What is $\sqrt{144}$?

   A. 10
   B. 11
   C. 12
   D. 14

6. Write the number four million as the product of a single digit and a power of 10.

   Answer: _____

TIP of the DAY

Writing a number as a product of a single digit and a power of 10 is using the scientific notation form.

WEEK 4 : DAY 4

1. Which of the following results in a rational number?

   A. $\sqrt[3]{148}$
   B. $\sqrt[3]{36}$
   C. $\sqrt[3]{49}$
   D. $\sqrt[3]{125}$

2. Write the number thirty-four thousand as the product of a single digit and a power of 10.

   A. 3.4×10^3
   B. 3.4×10^4
   C. 3.4×10^5
   D. 3.4×10^6

3. Which expression is true?

   A. $7,642 = 76.42 \times 10^3$
   B. $84,700 = 8.47 \times 10^4$
   C. $635 = 6.35 \times 10^5$
   D. $59,300 = 5.93 \times 10^5$

4. Which of the following numbers is the greatest in value?

   A. 6×10^6
   B. 4.39×10^7
   C. 5.465×10^5
   D. 3.6×10^8

5. Find the product of the numbers:

   $$(4 \times 10^3)(5 \times 10^6)$$

   Answer: _____

6. Find the quotient of the numbers:

   $$(3.5 \times 10^6) \div (7 \times 10^3)$$

   Answer: _____

TIP of the DAY

We use scientific notation to express numbers that are too big or too small.

33

WEEK 4 : DAY 5

ASSESSMENT

1. Which of the following numbers is the least in value?

   A. 9.1×10^4
   B. 3.4×10^6
   C. 6.81×10^7
   D. 1.2×10^5

   8.EE.A.2 & 8.EE.A.3

2. Write the number fifty-six million as the product of a single digit and a power of 10.

   A. 5.6×10^4
   B. 5.6×10^5
   C. 5.6×10^6
   D. 5.6×10^7

   8.EE.A.2 & 8.EE.A.3

3. How many times is the number 6×10^7 greater than the number 2×10^5?

   A. 30
   B. 300
   C. 3,000
   D. 3,0000

   8.EE.A.2 & 8.EE.A.3

4. How many times is the number 4×10^{12} smaller than the number 16×10^{16}?

   A. 400
   B. 4,000
   C. 40,000
   D. 400,000

   8.EE.A.2 & 8.EE.A.3

5. The mass of Earth is 6.0×10^{21} tons. The mass of Jupiter is 1.9×10^{24} tons. How many times is the mass of Jupiter greater than the mass of Earth rounded to the nearest whole number?

   Answer: _____

   8.EE.A.2 & 8.EE.A.3

6. The distance from the Sun to Earth is 1.496×10^8 km. The distance from the Sun to Saturn is 1.429×10^9 km. How many times is Earth closer to the Sun than Saturn is? Round to the nearest whole number.

   Answer: _____

   8.EE.A.2 & 8.EE.A.3

DAY 6
Challenge question

What is $\sqrt{\sqrt[3]{64}}$?

Answer: _____

8.EE.A.2 & 8.EE.A.3

34

WEEK 5

Week 5 is all about numbers that are expressed in the form of a single digit multiplied by an integer power of 10. Don't let that confuse you! We will be working with scientific notation.

You can find detailed video explanations of each problem in the book by visiting:
ArgoPrep.com/ccm8

WEEK 5 : DAY 1

1. Which of the following numbers represents 4.32×10^{12}?

   A. 432,000,000
   B. 432,000,000,000
   C. 4,320,000,000
   D. 4,320,000,000,000

2. What is 35 trillion expressed in scientific notation?

   A. 3.5×10^{12}
   B. 3.5×10^{13}
   C. 3.5×10^{9}
   D. 3.5×10^{15}

3. Express $(3 \times 10^5)(5 \times 10^7)$ in scientific notation.

   A. 15×10^{12}
   B. 15×10^{3}
   C. 1.5×10^{12}
   D. 1.5×10^{13}

4. The area of Pacific Ocean is 161,800 sq km. Express the area of the Pacific Ocean in scientific notation.

   Answer: _____

5. Express the number 3.785×10^{-6} in decimals.

   Answer: _____

6. Which of the following numbers represents 5.39×10^{-6}?

   A. 0.00000539
   B. 0.0000539
   C. 0.000539
   D. 0.00539

TIP of the DAY

When working with scientific notation, positive exponents indicate you need to move the decimal point to the right, which will make the number bigger in value. Negative exponents indicate you need to move the decimal point to the left, which will make the number smaller in value.

WEEK 5 : DAY 2

1. Which of the following numbers represents 7.11×10^8?

   A. 711,000,000
   B. 7,110,000,000
   C. 71,100,000,000
   D. 7,110,000

   8.EE.A.4 & 8.EE.A.5

2. Express $(7.1 \times 10^{-3})(4 \times 10^{-6})$ in scientific notation.

   A. 28.4×10^{-8}
   B. 28.4×10^{-10}
   C. 2.84×10^{-8}
   D. 2.84×10^{-9}

   8.EE.A.4 & 8.EE.A.5

3. What is 0.0000036 expressed in scientific notation?

   A. 3.6×10^{-5}
   B. 3.6×10^{-6}
   C. 3.6×10^{-7}
   D. 3.6×10^{-8}

   8.EE.A.4 & 8.EE.A.5

4. Express $(8.4 \times 10^3) \div (2.0 \times 10^8)$ in scientific notation.

   A. 4.2×10^{11}
   B. 4.2×10^5
   C. 4.2×10^{-5}
   D. 4.2×10^{-11}

   8.EE.A.4 & 8.EE.A.5

5. Mount Everest is approximately 29,000 ft. in height. Express the height of Mount Everest in scientific notation.

   Answer: _____

   8.EE.A.4 & 8.EE.A.5

6. The density of seawater is 0.00103 *kilo/cm³*. Express this number in scientific notation.

   Answer: _____

   8.EE.A.4 & 8.EE.A.5

TIP of the DAY

Numbers written in scientific form are in the format $m \times 10^n$ where m is any real number and n is an exponent.

WEEK 5 : DAY 3

1. What is 476 billion expressed in scientific notation?

   A. 4.76×10^{12}
   B. 4.76×10^{11}
   C. 4.76×10^{8}
   D. 4.76×10^{9}

   8.EE.A.4 & 8.EE.A.5

2. What is 0.00675 expressed in scientific notation?

   A. 675×10^{-2}
   B. 6.75×10^{-3}
   C. 6.75×10^{-5}
   D. 6.75×10^{3}

   8.EE.A.4 & 8.EE.A.5

3. Carbon-12 atom's mass is approximately $1.66 \times 10^{-24} g$. Express this number in kilos.

   Answer: _____

   8.EE.A.4 & 8.EE.A.5

4. What is the slope of the line on the graph shown below?

   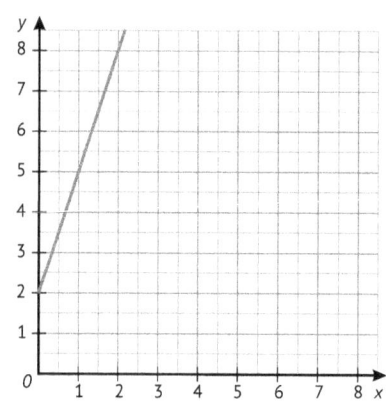

   A. 1   B. 2   C. 3   D. 4

   8.EE.A.4 & 8.EE.A.5

5. What is the slope of the line on the graph shown below?

   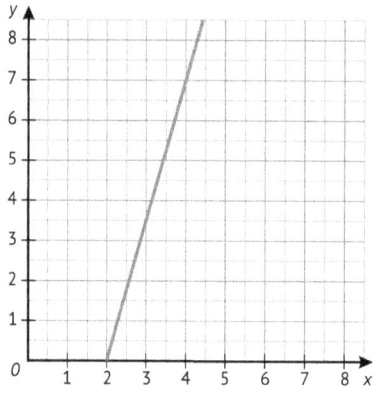

   Answer: _____

   8.EE.A.4 & 8.EE.A.5

TIP of the DAY

Do you remember the slope formula? Determine the change in y over the change in x to calculate the slope of a line.

WEEK 5 : DAY 4

1. Which of the following lines has a slope of 5?

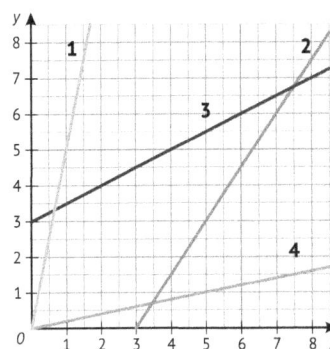

   A. 1   B. 2   C. 3   D. 4

   8.EE.A.4 & 8.EE.A.5

2. The graph below shows the height of a tree as time passes. At what speed does this tree grow?

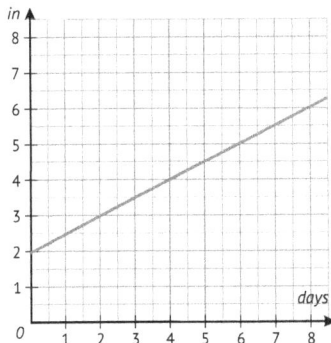

   A. 0.2 in per day   C. 1 in per day
   B. 0.5 in per day   D. 2 in per day

   8.EE.A.4 & 8.EE.A.5

3. Which of the following equations describes the relationship of distance vs. time on the graph shown below?

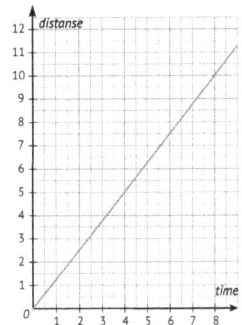

   A. $y = 8x$
   B. $y = \frac{8}{10}x$
   C. $y = \frac{10}{8}x$
   D. $y = 10x$

   8.EE.A.4 & 8.EE.A.5

4. In a period of six hours, the air temperature rose from 68°F to 77°F. If we were to graph this change, what would the slope be on the graph?

   Answer: _____

   8.EE.A.4 & 8.EE.A.5

5. The lines on the graph show the amount of problems that Molly and Cindy solved in one week. How many times faster does Molly solve problems than Cindy?

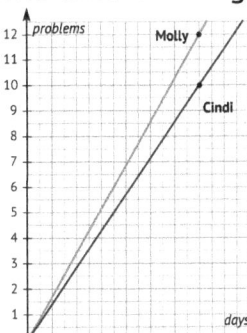

   Answer: _____

   8.EE.A.4 & 8.EE.A.5

TIP of the DAY

You have probably heard of the phrase «rise over run» which is the slope of the line. A slope of a line tells us the direction and steepness.

39

WEEK 5 : DAY 5

ASSESSMENT

1. Which line on the graph corresponds to the equation $8 = 4t$?

   A. 1   C. 3
   B. 2   D. 4

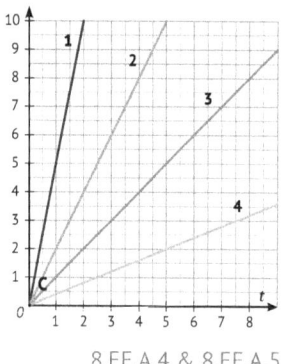

8.EE.A.4 & 8.EE.A.5

2. How many times greater is the slope of line 1 than the slope of line 2?

   A. 2.5   C. 5.5
   B. 3   D. 6

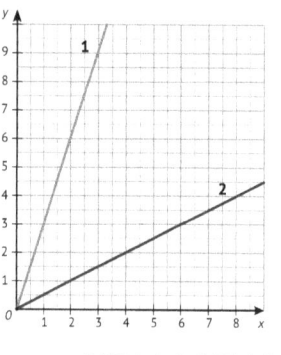

8.EE.A.4 & 8.EE.A.5

3. The graph shows the speed of two cars. How much time does it take for car 2 to travel the distance that car 1 travels in 3 hours?

   A. 3   C. 4.5
   B. 4   D. 5

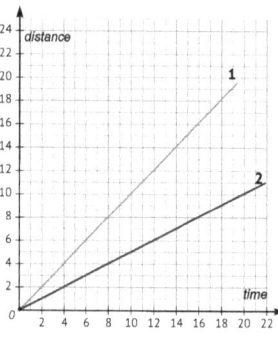

8.EE.A.4 & 8.EE.A.5

4. Matthew has two puppies. The first one gains 0.5 oz per week and another one gains weight 2 times faster than the first. Use the graph shown on the right and draw two lines to represent the weight gain of the puppies.

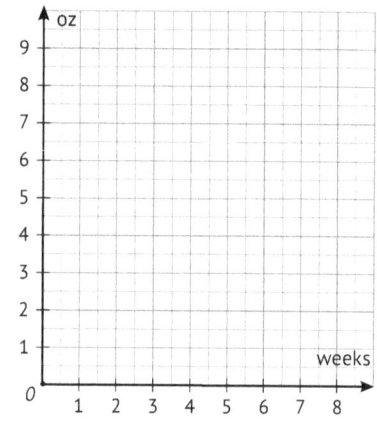

8.EE.A.4 & 8.EE.A.5

5. What is the slope of a line segment that has the endpoints (1,3) and (3,8)?

   A. 2   C. 2.5
   B. 3   D. 5

8.EE.A.4 & 8.EE.A.5

6. Find the slope of a line segment that has the endpoints (3,2) and (4,9)?

   A. 3   C. 7
   B. 5   D. 9

8.EE.A.4 & 8.EE.A.5

DAY 6
Challenge question

Express $(7.6 \times 10^{-5}) + (2.0 \times 10^{-14})$ in scientific notation.

8.EE.A.4 & 8.EE.A.5

40

WEEK 6

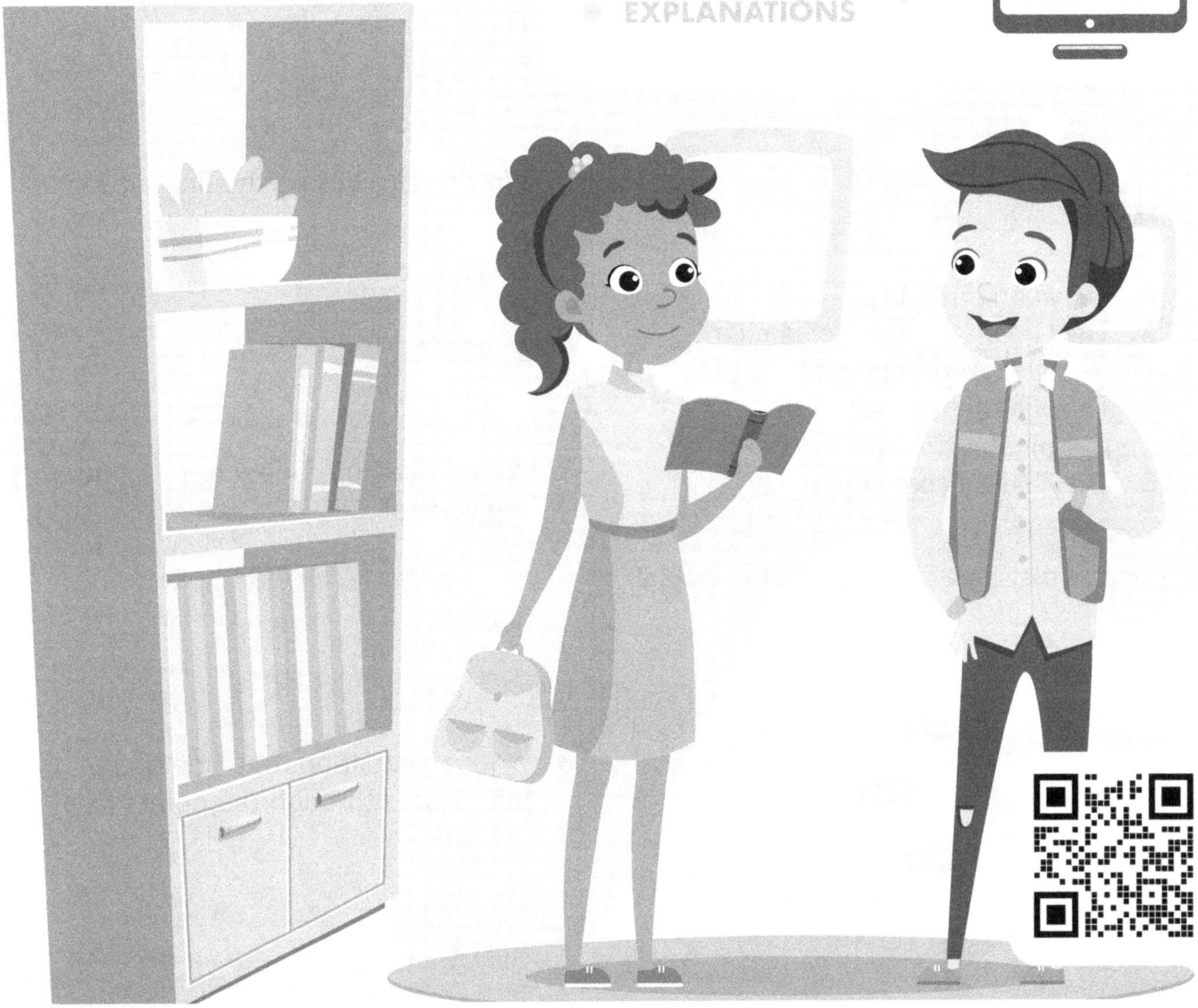

In this week we will use similar triangles to understand why the slope is the same between any two distinct points on a coordinate plane. We will also solve linear equations with one variable.

You can find detailed video explanations of each problem in the book by visiting: ArgoPrep.com/ccm8

WEEK 6 : DAY 1

1. Why do the line segments $\overline{AB}$ and $\overline{BC}$ have the same slope?

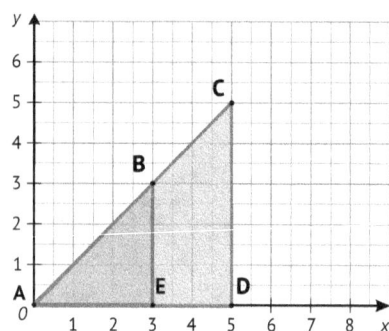

   A. They don't intercept
   B. They lie on the sides of similar triangles $\triangle ABE$ and $\triangle ACD$
   C. They lie on the hypotenuse of a rectangular triangle
   D. They have a common point

   8.EE.B.6 & 8.EE.C.7

2. What is the slope of the line on the graph?

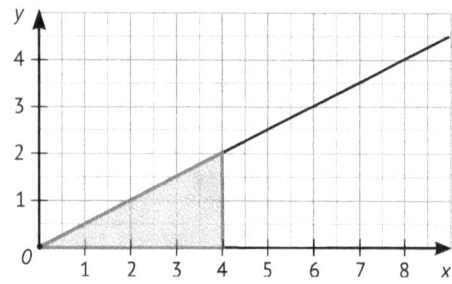

   A. $\dfrac{1}{2}$ B. 1   C. $\dfrac{3}{2}$ D. 2

   8.EE.B.6 & 8.EE.C.7

3. What is the slope of the line $y = -8x + 6$?

   A. 6
   B. 8
   C. -6
   D. -8

   8.EE.B.6 & 8.EE.C.7

4. Which point lies on the line $y = 3x$?

   A. (2, 5)
   B. (3, 6)
   C. (4, 12)
   D. (8, 20)

   8.EE.B.6 & 8.EE.C.7

5. Where does the line $y = 8 - 3x$ intercept the vertical axis y?

   Answer: _____

   8.EE.B.6 & 8.EE.C.7

6. Write an equation for a line on the graph that passes through the points (0, 4) and (12, 16).

   Answer: _____

   8.EE.B.6 & 8.EE.C.7

TIP of the DAY

The standard equation of a line is written as $y = mx + b$.

42

WEEK 6 : DAY 2

1. Determine the slope of the line.

   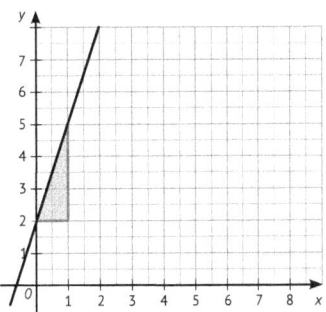

   A. 1   B. 2   C. 3   D. 4

   8.EE.B.6 & 8.EE.C.7

2. Write an equation for a line through the origin on the graph.

   A. $y = 3x$
   B. $y = \dfrac{4}{3}x$
   C. $y = 4x$
   D. $y = \dfrac{3}{4}x$

   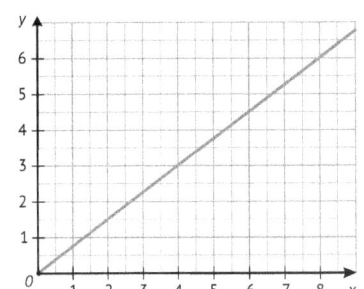

   8.EE.B.6 & 8.EE.C.7

3. Solve the linear equation $10 - 2x = 0$.

   A. 4
   B. 5
   C. 6
   D. 8

   8.EE.B.6 & 8.EE.C.7

4. Which equation gives us a value of 6 for x?

   A. $5x - 7 = 3 + 7x$
   B. $8 - 4x = 3x + 5$
   C. $6x + 12 = 12x - 24$
   D. $10x - 32 = 6x + 16$

   8.EE.B.6 & 8.EE.C.7

5. Where does the line $y = 4x - 5$ intercept the vertical axis y?

   Answer: _____

   8.EE.B.6 & 8.EE.C.7

6. What is the slope of the line that passes through the points (2, 6) and (3, 9)?

   Answer: _____

   8.EE.B.6 & 8.EE.C.7

TIP of the DAY

When you are given two points on a line, you can always find the equation of the line. First calculate the slope. Then you can use the formula: $y - y_1 = m(x - x_1)$.

WEEK 6 : DAY 3

1. Write an equation for the line on the graph.

   A. $y = 6x + 2$
   B. $y = 2x + 6$
   C. $y = 4x + 2$
   D. $y = 6x - 2$

   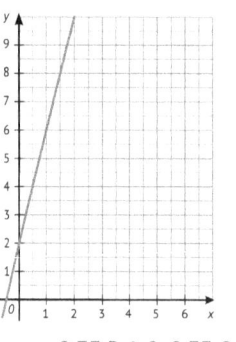

2. Write an equation for the line on the graph.

   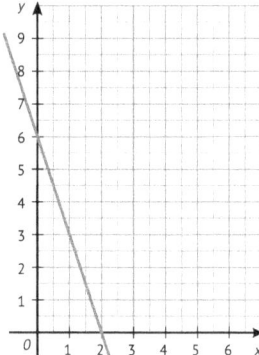

   Answer: _____

3. Solve the linear equation $5x + 15 = 4x - 10$.

   A. 25
   B. -5
   C. 5
   D. -25

4. Which equation gives us a value of 8 for x?

   A. $2x + 14 = 4x - 2$
   B. $5x - 10 = 3x$
   C. $4x + 25 = 8x + 12$
   D. $2x = 4x + 16$

5. Write an equation for the line on the graph.

   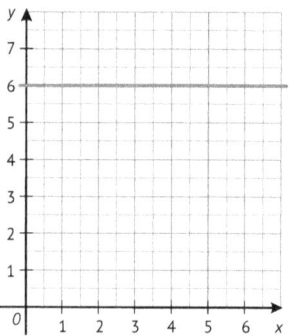

   Answer: _____

6. Solve the linear equation

   $$\frac{2}{5}x + 25 = \frac{4}{2}x + 30$$

   A. 3.25
   B. -3.125
   C. 325
   D. -32.5

TIP of the DAY

When solving equations, remember to perform the operations on both sides of the equation. If you multiply one side of the equation by 5, you need to multiply the other side of the equation by 5 too.

WEEK 6 : DAY 4

1. Solve the linear equation $\frac{3}{5}x + 10 = \frac{4}{5}x - 6$

   A. 80
   B. -80
   C. 8
   D. -8

2. Which of the following equations does not have a solution?

   A. $2x + 5 - 4x = 6x + 3$
   B. $5x + 5 + 4x = 6x + 3$
   C. $2x + 5 + 4x = 6x + 3$
   D. $8x + 5 + 4x = 16x + 3$

3. Which equation gives us a value of 10 for x?

   A. $4x + 20 = 6x - 50$
   B. $25x + 10 = 15x - 10$
   C. $20x - 20 = 10x - 30$
   D. $20 - 6x = \frac{2}{5}x - 44$

4. Which equation has an unending quantity of solutions?

   A. $6x + 8 = 12x + 8 - 6x$
   B. $5x + 7 = 13x - 7 - 7x$
   C. $2x - 8 - 2x = 6 + 2x$
   D. $4x - 6 = 4x + 6$

5. Solve the linear equation

   $15x + 46 - 2x = 4(3x + 4) + x + 30$

   Answer: _____

6. What is the value of x in the equation

   $\frac{5}{3}x - 4 = \frac{7}{3}x - 5$?

   Answer: _____

When solving equations, first try to isolate the term that contains the variable.

WEEK 6 : DAY 5

ASSESSMENT

1. Solve the linear equation

   $5(2x + 2) = 2(5x + 5)$

   A. 5
   B. 15
   C. 4
   D. Has an unending quantity of solutions

   8.EE.B.6 & 8.EE.C.7

2. Which equation has an unending quantity of solutions?

   A. $5x + 6 = 5x + 6 - x$
   B. $6(2x + 4) = 16x + 2(x + 12)$
   C. $12 + 3x = 14 + 5x - 2$
   D. $6x - 3 = 16 - 10$

   8.EE.B.6 & 8.EE.C.7

3. Which of the following equations does not have a solution?

   A. $x + 3 - 4x = 4(x - 3)$
   B. $6x + 2 - 2x = 6x + 2$
   C. $5x + 4 = 7x - 8$
   D. $6(x + 2) - 2x = 4(x - 3)$

   8.EE.B.6 & 8.EE.C.7

4. Solve the linear equation

   $9x - 19 = 2(2x - 7) - 5 + 5x$

   A. 9
   B. 6
   C. Does not have a solution
   D. Has an unending quantity of solutions

   8.EE.B.6 & 8.EE.C.7

5. Solve the linear equation

   $3(x - 8) + 2x = 76$

   A. 18
   B. 20
   C. 22
   D. 25

   8.EE.B.6 & 8.EE.C.7

6. Solve the linear equation

   $10x + 25 = 5(2x + 12) + 1$

   Answer: _____

   8.EE.B.6 & 8.EE.C.7

DAY 6
Challenge question

Solve the equation $x\sqrt{6} - 2 = 0$

_____

8.EE.B.6 & 8.EE.C.7

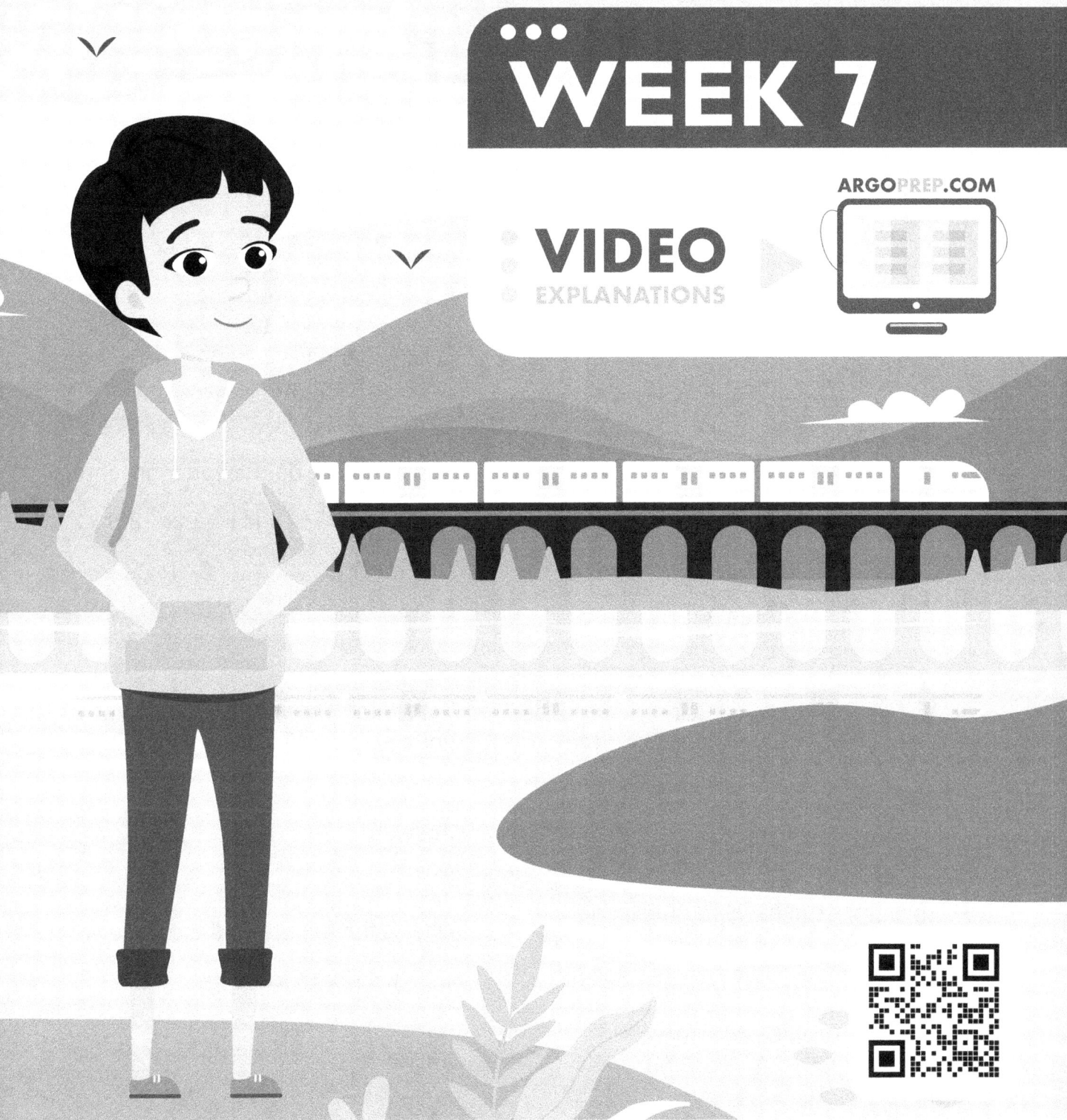

Week 7 is all about working with two linear equations and understanding how to solve for the points of intersections.

You can find detailed video explanations of each problem in the book by visiting: ArgoPrep.com/ccm8

WEEK 7 : DAY 1

1. Which two linear equations correspond to the lines on the graph?

   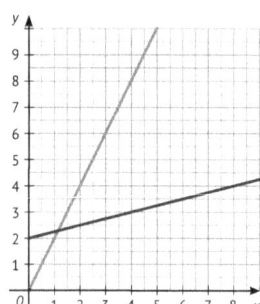

   A. $y = 2x$ and $y = 2 + \frac{1}{2}x$

   B. $y = 2x$ and $y = 2 + \frac{1}{4}x$

   C. $y = \frac{1}{2}x$ and $y = 2 + \frac{1}{4}x$

   D. $y = 2x$ and $y = 2 + 4x$

   8.EE.C.8

2. Which statement is FALSE?

   A. Two lines have one intersection point.
   B. Two lines can have no intersection points.
   C. Two lines can have two intersection points.
   D. Two lines can be congruent.

   8.EE.C.8

3. What is the solution to the equations

   $y = 10x + 4$ and $y = 11x + 2$?

   A. $x = 1$ and $y = 4$
   B. $x = 2$ and $y = 12$
   C. $x = 2$ and $y = 24$
   D. $x = 12$ and $y = 4$

   8.EE.C.8

4. At what point do the equations intersect

   $y = 120 - 6x$ and $y = 14x + 80$?

   A. (4, 12)   C. (5, 16)
   B. (2, 108)   D. (10, 120)

   8.EE.C.8

5. Determine the intersection point of the lines $y = 4x + 12$ and $2y = 8x + 24$?

   Answer: _____

   8.EE.C.8

6. What is the solution to the equations

   $y = 18x + 25$ and $y = -6x - 23$?

   Answer: _____

   8.EE.C.8

Always make sure to reread word problems and underline the relevant information.

WEEK 7 : DAY 2

1. Which two linear equations correspond to the lines on the graph.

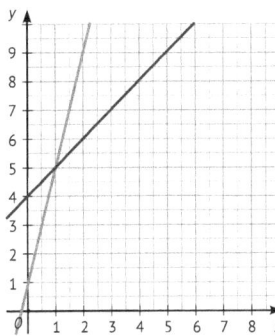

   A. $y = 4x + 1$ and $y = x + 4$
   B. $y = 2x + 1$ and $y = x + 2$
   C. $y = 4x + 2$ and $y = 2x + 1$
   D. $y = 2x + 2$ and $y = x + 2$

   8.EE.C.8

2. What is the point of intersection of the two lines shown below?

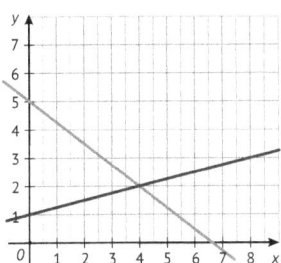

   A. (2, 4)   C. (4, 2)
   B. (2, 2)   D. (4, 4)

   8.EE.C.8

3. When two lines intersect on the graph that means:

   A. Two linear equations have a solution.
   B. Two linear equations have NO solution.
   C. Two linear equations are the same.
   D. It's impossible.

   8.EE.C.8

4. Find the solutions to the equations
   $$y = 8x - 6 \text{ and } y = 4x + 14?$$

   A. $x = 5$ and $y = 34$
   B. $x = 4$ and $y = 32$
   C. $x = 24$ and $y = 5$
   D. $x = 15$ and $y = 34$

   8.EE.C.8

5. Sam rode a motorbike for 3 hours and Joshua rode a bike for 2 hours. Determine at what speed everyone rode, if it's known that they traveled 80 miles together, and Sam rode twice as fast as Joshua.

   A. Sam rode 10 mph, Joshua rode 20 mph
   B. Sam rode 40 mph, Joshua rode 20 mph
   C. Sam rode 20 mph, Joshua rode 10 mph
   D. Sam rode 10 mph, Joshua rode 20 mph

   8.EE.C.8

If you are stuck on a multiple choice question, using the plug and check method can be a great strategy.

49

WEEK 7 : DAY 3

1. The lines $y = \frac{1}{2}x + 3$ and $y = 4x - 4$ intersect at which point?

   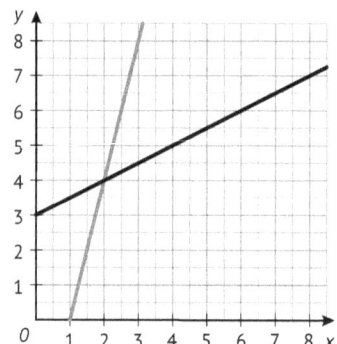

   A. $x = 1$ and $y = 3$
   B. $x = 4$ and $y = 2$
   C. $x = 3$ and $y = 1$
   D. $x = 2$ and $y = 4$

   8.EE.C.8

2. When two lines do NOT intersect on the graph that means:

   A. Two linear equations have a solution.
   B. Two linear equations have NO solution.
   C. Two linear equations are the same
   D. It's impossible.

   8.EE.C.8

3. At what point do the equations intersect

   $y = 25x + 54$ and $y = 15x + 14$?

   A. (4, 16)   C. (-6, 12)
   B. (14, 18)   D. (-4, -46)

   8.EE.C.8

4. Seven kittens and 5 puppies eat 87 oz of food per day. How much food does each pet eat if each kitten gets 3 oz less than each puppy?

   A. Each kitten gets 6 oz and each puppy gets 9 oz
   B. Each kitten gets 9 oz and each puppy gets 6 oz
   C. Each kitten gets 7 oz and each puppy gets 10 oz
   D. Each kitten gets 8 oz and each puppy gets 6 oz

   8.EE.C.8

5. A café sold twice as many lattes as cappuccinos. How many cups of each drink were sold, if they sold 72 cups in total?

   Answer: _____

   8.EE.C.8

If you are unsure of the correct answer, be sure to eliminate the answer choices you know that are incorrect. Making educated guesses will increase your chances of answering the question correctly.

50

WEEK 7 : DAY 4

1. What is the solution to the equations $2x = 2(y - 2)$ and $x - 4 = \dfrac{4y}{12}$?

   A. $x = 6$ and $y = 5$
   B. $x = 4$ and $y = 8$
   C. $x = 7$ and $y = 9$
   D. $x = 8$ and $y = 12$

   8.EE.C.8

2. Find the equations to the two lines shown on the graph below.

   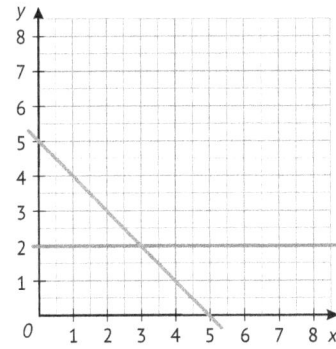

   A. $y = 5 + x$ and $y = 2$
   B. $y = 5 - x$ and $y = 2$
   C. $y = 5x - 5$ and $y = x$
   D. $y = 5x - 2$ and $y = x$

   8.EE.C.8

3. A certain restaurant sold burgers for $14 and steak for $25. The restaurant sold a total of $534 worth of burgers and steak on Monday. How many burgers and steaks were sold if the steaks were ordered three times more than the burgers?

   Answer: _____

   8.EE.C.8

4. Mr. Sheldon planted two trees that were 30 inches and 20 inches in height. The first tree grows 2 inches per week, and the second tree grows 3 inches per week. In how many weeks will the trees be the same height?

   A. 5 weeks
   B. 10 weeks
   C. 15 weeks
   D. 20 weeks

   8.EE.C.8

5. Fifteen bales of hay were loaded into a truck. Some of the bales weighed 150 pounds, and some weighed 100 pounds. How many bales of 100 pounds and 150 pounds were loaded into the truck, if their total weight is 1,900 pounds?

   Answer: _____

   8.EE.C.8

When working with word problems, it is always a good idea to underline the keywords.

WEEK 7 : DAY 5

ASSESSMENT

1. In a shoe store 110 pairs of shoes were packed in the boxes. Shoes for adults were packed 6 pairs in a box, and children's shoes were packed 10 pairs in a box. How many boxes were used, if shoes for adults took 5 boxes more than children's shoes?

   A. 12 boxes
   B. 13 boxes
   C. 14 boxes
   D. 15 boxes

   8.EE.C.8

2. Issac, Benjamin, and Howard arranged a train journey. Howard was late for the train and left by car two hours later. In how many hours will Howard catch up to the train if the train goes 50 mph and his car goes 60 mph?

   A. 8 hours
   B. 10 hours
   C. 12 hours
   D. 14 hours

   8.EE.C.8

3. Ellie spent $100 on T-shirts and shorts. A pair of shorts costs $20. One T-shirt costs $5 cheaper than one pair of shorts. How many T-shirts and shorts did Ellie buy if she bought twice as many T-shirts as shorts?

   Answer: _____

   8.EE.C.8

4. One girl did not come to school on Monday, so the number of boys and girls was the same. Three boys did not come to school on Tuesday, so the number of boys was $\frac{3}{4}$ of the number of girls. How many boys and girls are in the school when no students are absent?

   A. 16 boys and 18 girls
   B. 14 boys and 17 girls
   C. 17 boys and 18 girls
   D. 15 boys and 16 girls

   8.EE.C.8

5. Mr. Brown has hens and goats. He has 30 animals in total. How many hens and goats does Mr. Brown have if there are 80 animal legs total?

   Answer: _____

   8.EE.C.8

6. The guys bought hamburgers and pizza for $90. Each hamburger costs $6 and each pizza costs $2. How many hamburgers and pizzas were bought if all the hamburgers they bought cost twice as much as all the pizzas they bought?

   A. 12 hamburgers and 14 pizzas
   B. 10 hamburgers and 15 pizzas
   C. 15 hamburgers and 12 pizzas
   D. 12 hamburgers and 16 pizzas

   8.EE.C.8

DAY 6
Challenge question

What is the solution to the equations
$3(x - y) + 4 = x + y$ and $2(y - x) + 11 = x + y$

Answer: _____

8.EE.C.8

WEEK 8

VIDEO EXPLANATIONS

In Week 8 we will be working with functions, inputs, outputs, and analyzing graphs.

You can find detailed video explanations of each problem in the book by visiting:
ArgoPrep.com/ccm8

WEEK 8 : DAY 1

1. Which set of points forms a function?

   A. (1, 2); (2, 4); (3, 6)
   B. (1, 2); (1, 4); (1, 6)
   C. (2, 2); (2, 6); (3, 6)
   D. (0, 5); (0, 4); (0, -1)

   8.F.A.1 & 8.F.A.2

2. Which statement is true?

   A. For a function each value of y corresponds to only one value of x.
   B. For a function each value of x corresponds to only one value of y.
   C. For a function there is an infinite number of values of y for each value of x.
   D. For a function there is no value of y for each value of x.

   8.F.A.1 & 8.F.A.2

3. What is NOT a function?

   A. $y = 3x + 5$
   B. $y = x$
   C. $y = 6$
   D. $x = 4$

   8.F.A.1 & 8.F.A.2

4. What functional relationship does the data in the chart show?

x	y
1	16
2	14
3	12
4	10

   Answer: _____

   8.F.A.1 & 8.F.A.2

5. There is a graph of a function in the drawing. What is the output when the input is 3?

   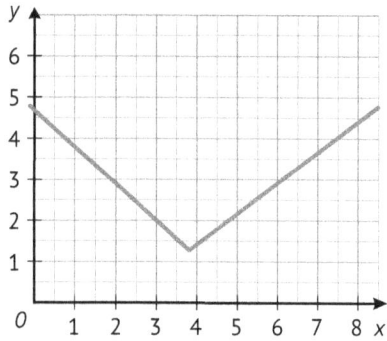

   Answer: _____

   8.F.A.1 & 8.F.A.2

TIP of the DAY

A function has a special relationship where each input is related to exactly one output.

WEEK 8 : DAY 2

1. Which of the following does NOT assign only one value of y to each value of x?

   A. $\dfrac{5}{y} = 7x + \dfrac{10}{2y}$
   B. $y = 45 - 9x$
   C. $8y = 32x^2$
   D. $yx = 14$

   8.F.A.1 & 8.F.A.2

2. Which set of points does NOT form a function?

   A. (1, 2); (2, 4); (3, 6)
   B. (5, 4); (0, 0); (-1, 7)
   C. (5, 2); (5, 6); (5, 5)
   D. (0, 3); (-2, -4); (2, -4)

   8.F.A.1 & 8.F.A.2

Cameron and Robert solve word problems. Cameron solves 6 word problems a day and Robert solves 4 word problems a day. Robert has already solved 20 word problems.

3. In a week, who will have solved more word problems?

   A. Cameron will solve 6 word problems more than Robert.
   B. Robert will solve 6 word problems more than Cameron.
   C. Robert will solve 10 word problems more than Cameron.
   D. They will solve an equal number of word problems.

   8.F.A.1 & 8.F.A.2

4. In 2 weeks, who will solve more word problems?

   A. Cameron will solve 8 word problems more than Robert.
   B. Robert will solve 2 word problems more than Cameron.
   C. Robert will solve 6 word problems fewer than Cameron.
   D. They will solve an equal number of word problems.

   8.F.A.1 & 8.F.A.2

5. Looking at the table below, can this form a function?

x	y
1	10
2	11
3	12
4	14

   Answer: _____

   8.F.A.1 & 8.F.A.2

TIP of the DAY

You can determine whether a set of points forms a function by analyzing the inputs and outputs. If one input has more than one output, you know that is not a function.

WEEK 8 : DAY 3

1. If the output is -2, what is the input in the function on the graph?

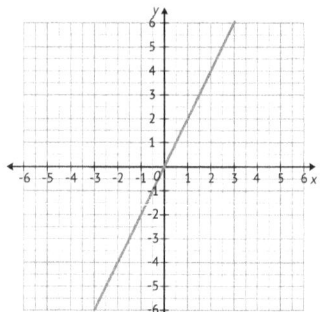

   Answer: _____

   8.F.A.1 & 8.F.A.2

2. Which of the following equations is NOT a function?

   A. $2y = 5y - 10x$
   B. $25 - 4y = 56x$
   C. $15x + 4y = 2(2y + 7)$
   D. $34x = \dfrac{84}{y}$

   8.F.A.1 & 8.F.A.2

3. The equation of a function is $y = 12x - 7$. What is the output when the input is 5?

   A. 50   C. 56
   B. 53   D. 60

   8.F.A.1 & 8.F.A.2

4. Christie and Susan save money for summer vacation. Christie saves $10 each week. The diagram shows how much money Susan saves. Who will save more money by the end of the 10 week summer?

   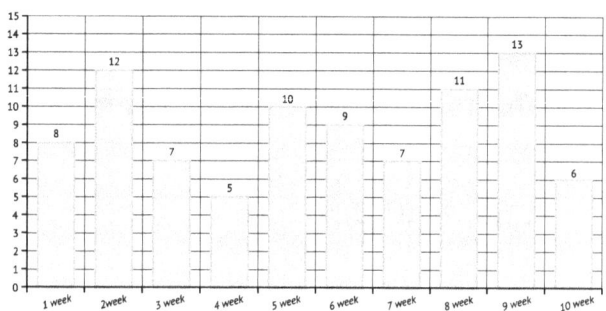

   A. Christie will save $20 more than Susan.
   B. Susan will save $10 more than Christie.
   C. Christie will save $12 more than Susan.
   D. They will save an equal amount.

   8.F.A.1 & 8.F.A.2

5. The equation of a function is $y = 60 - x^2$. How will the value of y change, if the value of x will change from 4 to 6?

   Answer: _____

   8.F.A.1 & 8.F.A.2

TIP of the DAY

Pay attention to the variables and what they represent.

WEEK 8 : DAY 4

1. If the output is -1, what was the input in the function on the graph?

   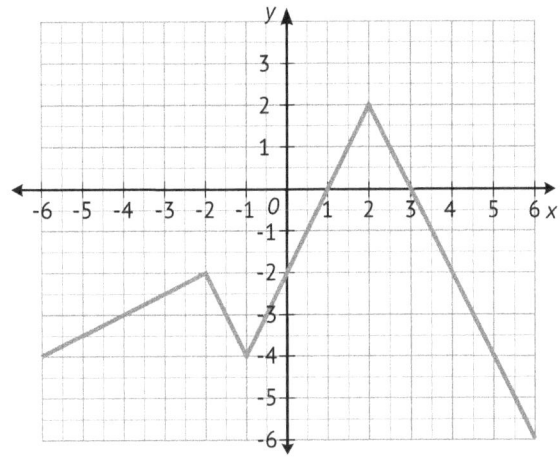

   Answer: _____

   8.F.A.1 & 8.F.A.2

2. The equation of a function is $y = 14 - 6x$. If the output is -4, what was the input?

   A. 3
   B. -4
   C. -3
   D. 4

   8.F.A.1 & 8.F.A.2

Dr. Hillford is tracking the weight of specimen A and specimen B. Every week she weighs them and writes the data into the charts.

Specimen A		Specimen B	
1st week	100 oz	1st week	120 oz
2nd week	108 oz	2nd week	126 oz
3rd week	116 oz	3rd week	132 oz
4th week	124 oz	4th week	138 oz
5th week	132 oz	5th week	144 oz
6th week	140 oz	6th week	150 oz
7th week	148 oz	7th week	156 oz

3. Which specimen gains weight faster?

   Answer: _____

   8.F.A.1 & 8.F.A.2

4. In how many weeks will specimen A and B be at the same weight?

   A. 11 weeks
   B. 12 weeks
   C. 13 weeks
   D. 14 weeks

   8.F.A.1 & 8.F.A.2

5. The equation of a function is $y = \dfrac{18}{x} + 10$. What is the output when the input is -3?

   A. 4
   B. 3
   C. -4
   D. -3

   8.F.A.1 & 8.F.A.2

TIP of the DAY

$y = x^2$
Is this a linear function or nonlinear function? This is a parabola and parabolas are nonlinear functions!

WEEK 8 : DAY 5

ASSESSMENT

1. The equation of a function is $y = 2\sqrt{x} + 16$. If the output is 16, what was the input?

   A. 16
   B. 8
   C. 1
   D. 0

   8.F.A.1 & 8.F.A.2

2. The equation of a function is $y = 4x + 10$. How should the value of x change, to change the value of y from 42 to -6?

   Answer: _____

   8.F.A.1 & 8.F.A.2

3. The equation of a function is $y = 2(8 + 4x)$. How much will the value of y increase, if the value of x will increase by one?

   A. 6
   B. 7
   C. 8
   D. 10

   8.F.A.1 & 8.F.A.2

The graphs show the number of people who watched Movie A and Movie B over a period of 7 days.

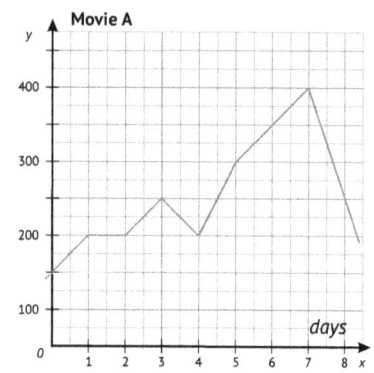

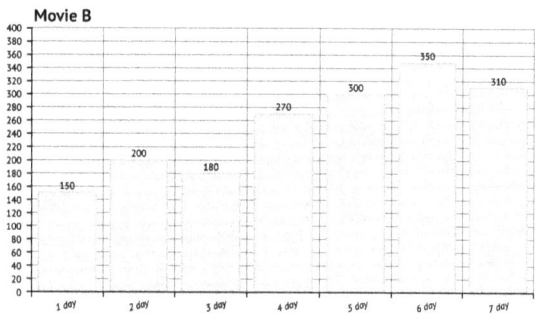

4. How many more people watched Movie A than Movie B over the period of 7 days?

   Answer: _____

   8.F.A.1 & 8.F.A.2

5. How many people watched Movie A over the period of 7 days?

   Answer: _____

   8.F.A.1 & 8.F.A.2

DAY 6
Challenge question

The equation of a function is $y = \dfrac{100}{x^2} - 30$. If the output is -26, what was the input?

_____

8.F.A.1 & 8.F.A.2

In Week 9 we continue to work with functions. You will learn whether or not a given equation is a linear function. We will also construct functions on a graph.

You can find detailed video explanations of each problem in the book by visiting: ArgoPrep.com/ccm8

WEEK 9 : DAY 1

1. Which of the following expressions is a linear function?

   A. $y = \dfrac{4}{3x} + 10$
   B. $y = 23 - 12x$
   C. $y = 6x^3$
   D. $y = 4\sqrt{x}$

2. Which set of points forms a linear function?

   A. (1, 5); (2, 10); (3, 15)
   B. (2, 3); (4, 15); (6, 18)
   C. (4, 4); (5, 6); (6, 7)
   D. (0, 10); (3, 15); (5, 20)

3. Which of the following expressions is a line, but is NOT a function?

   A. $y = 32 - x$
   B. $y = 5$
   C. $x = 23 + 4y$
   D. $x = 12$

4. What is the rate of change of a linear function that has points (0, 7) and (4, 23)?

   A. 4 C. 6
   B. 5 D. 7

5. A linear function has the rate of change of 4 and point (3, 18). What is the y-intercept of this function?

   Answer: _____

6. Five baseball cards were gifted to Jack and he decided to start a baseball collection. Every month Jack adds 2 baseball cards to his collection.

   A. What is the rate of change that describes the relationship between the quantity of Jack's baseball cards and time?

   Answer: _____

   B. What is the initial value of the function?

   Answer: _____

TIP of the DAY

An equation has the coordinates (1, 2) and (1, 4). Is the equation a function? As you can see the input «1» has more than one output. In this case the output is 2 and 4. Therefore, this equation is not a function.

60

WEEK 9 : DAY 2

1. Which of the following expressions is a linear function?

   A. $y = 342 - \dfrac{x}{2}$

   B. $y = 3 + \dfrac{3x^2}{4}$

   C. $y = -10\sqrt{x}$

   D. $y = \dfrac{x}{x^2}$

   8.F.A.3 & 8.F.B.4

2. Which set of points does NOT lay on the function $y = 5x - 2$?

   A. (1, 3); (2, 8); (10, 48)
   B. (-6, -32); (15, 73); (-10, -48)
   C. (4, 18); (-3, -17); (110, 548)
   D. (7, 33); (-16, -82); (-5, -27)

   8.F.A.3 & 8.F.B.4

3. What is the rate of change of a linear function that has the points (5, 10) and (7, 15)?

   A. 2
   B. $2\dfrac{1}{2}$
   C. 3
   D. $3\dfrac{1}{2}$

   8.F.A.3 & 8.F.B.4

4. What is the rate of change of a linear function that has the equation $4x + y = 6$?

   A. 4
   B. 6
   C. -4
   D. $\dfrac{1}{3}$

   8.F.A.3 & 8.F.B.4

5. Construct a graph of a function that has the y-intercept of 3 and the rate of change $\dfrac{1}{5}$.

   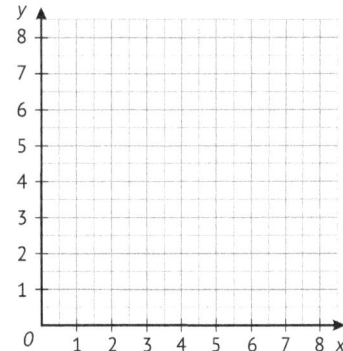

   8.F.A.3 & 8.F.B.4

6. Determine the slope and initial value of the function $y = -25 - 16x$.

   Answer: _____

   8.F.A.3 & 8.F.B.4

TIP of the DAY

The rate of change describes how one quantity changes in relation to the other quantity.

61

WEEK 9 : DAY 3

1. Which of the following expressions is a NONlinear function?

   A. $10 - y = 4x$ C. $y = x^2$

   B. $y = \dfrac{12 - x}{14}$ D. $y = \dfrac{3x + 4}{76}$

2. Which set of points does NOT form a linear function?

   A. (3, 6); (9, 18); (5, 10)
   B. (5, 3); (6, 1); (7, -1)
   C. (-1, 4); (2, 3); (7, 12)
   D. (3, 12); (5, 24); (7, 36)

3. What is the rate of change of the linear function that has the points (0, 7) and (4, 23)?

   A. 4
   B. 5
   C. 6
   D. 7

4. What is the rate of change of the linear function that has the equation $y = 13 - \dfrac{1}{3}x$?

   A. $-\dfrac{1}{3}$ C. 13

   B. 3   D. -3

5. Determine the rate of change of the function drawn on the graph.

   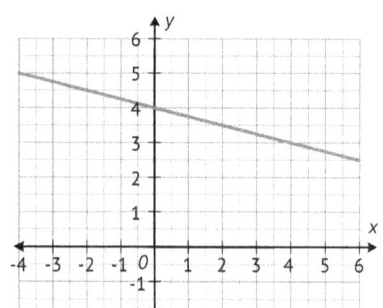

   Answer: _____

6. Determine the initial value of the function $y = 6x - 10$.

   Answer: _____

Practicing your math skills even 15 minutes a day at your home will greatly benefit you in the long run!

WEEK 9 : DAY 4

1. The linear function has the y-intercept of 5 and the point at (-4, -17). What is the rate of change?

   A. $2\frac{1}{2}$
   B. -5
   C. $5\frac{1}{2}$
   D. $-5\frac{1}{2}$

   8.F.A.3 & 8.F.B.4

2. Which of the following expressions is a NONlinear function?

   A. $y = x$
   B. $y = -6$
   C. $y = \frac{7x}{6}$
   D. $yx = 8$

   8.F.A.3 & 8.F.B.4

3. Which set of points does NOT lay on the function $y = 25 - 2x$?

   A. (3, 19); (8, 9); (-2, 29)
   B. (-3, 31); (-5, 35); (14, -3)
   C. (17, -9); (7, 11); (12, 1)
   D. (-9, 43); (-11, 46); (2, 21)

   8.F.A.3 & 8.F.B.4

4. Which point does NOT lay on the linear function $y = \frac{4x - 2}{5}$?

   A. (0, -0.4)
   B. (6, 4.4)
   C. (-8, -6)
   D. (5, 3.6)

   8.F.A.3 & 8.F.B.4

5. The chart shows the changes in the value of the deposit in a bank at the end of the year.

year	amount
1	$105
2	$110
3	$115
4	$120

   A. What is the rate of change of the function describing the relationship between the amount of the deposit and time?

   Answer: _____

   B. What is the initial value of the function?

   Answer: _____

   8.F.A.3 & 8.F.B.4

The initial value of a function is the point at which a function begins.

63

WEEK 9 : DAY 5

ASSESSMENT

1. What is the rate of change of the linear function that has the equation $y = 8x - 10$?

   A. $\dfrac{8}{10}$

   B. 8

   C. $\dfrac{10}{8}$

   D. 10

   8.F.A.3 & 8.F.B.4

2. Which of the following expressions is a NONlinear function?

   A. $y = \dfrac{2+1}{x} 2x$

   B. $y = \dfrac{2}{x}(x^2)$

   C. $y = \dfrac{4x}{3}(x)$

   D. $y = 3$

   8.F.A.3 & 8.F.B.4

3. The linear function has a y-intercept of 3 and the point at (6, 27). What is the rate of change?

   A. 1
   B. 2
   C. 3
   D. 4

   8.F.A.3 & 8.F.B.4

4. Which point does NOT lay on the linear function $y = 24 + 3x$?

   A. (4, 36)
   B. (14, 64)
   C. (-7, 3)
   D. (-8, 0)

   8.F.A.3 & 8.F.B.4

5. Determine the slope and the initial value of the function $y = -30 + x$.

   Answer: _____

   8.F.A.3 & 8.F.B.4

6. If a graph of a function changes the direction, it means that:

   A. The function is decreasing.
   B. The function is increasing.
   C. The function is NONlinear.
   D. The function has NO slope.

   8.F.A.3 & 8.F.B.4

DAY 6
Challenge question

Determine the initial value of the function which has the graph with points (-4, -7) and (8, 2).

_____

8.F.A.3 & 8.F.B.4

64

WEEK 10

In this week we will be looking at graphs to determine whether a function is increasing or decreasing and determine if it is a linear or nonlinear function.

You can find detailed video explanations of each problem in the book by visiting:
ArgoPrep.com/ccm8

WEEK 10 : DAY 1

1. Which graph is a linear function?

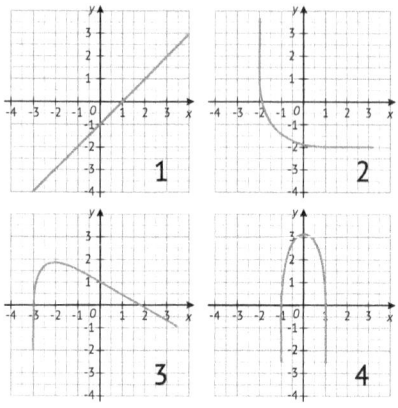

A. 1   B. 2   C. 3   D. 4

8.F.B.5

2. Which graph shows a linear function increasing?

A. 1   B. 2   C. 3   D. 4

8.F.B.5

3. How does the function drawn on the graph change?

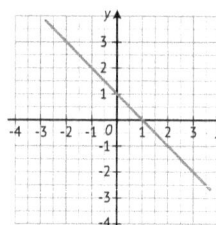

A. It is increasing
B. It is decreasing
C. It is changing its direction
D. It stays constant

8.F.B.5

4. How is the graph of the function changing in the equation $y = \dfrac{1}{2x} \times x^2$?

A. It is constantly decreasing.
B. It is constantly increasing.
C. It is changing its direction.
D. It is a horizontal line.

8.F.B.5

5. Is the value of the function $y = -25 - 16x$ decreasing or increasing if the value of x is increasing?

Answer: _____

8.F.B.5

TIP of the DAY

We can quickly tell if something is a function on a graph by using the vertical line test.

66

WEEK 10 : DAY 2

1. Which graph corresponds to a NONlinear function?

    A. 1
    B. 2
    C. 3
    D. 4

    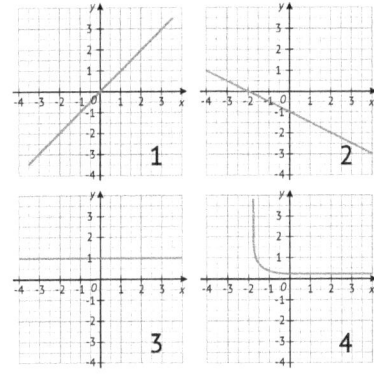

2. Which of the following functions is increasing constantly?

    A. $y = 4 - 3x$
    B. $y = -10 + 2x$
    C. $y = -2x^2$
    D. $y = -4(2 + x)$

3. How is the value of y changing on the graph when the value of x is increasing?

    A. It stays constant
    B. It is increasing
    C. It is decreasing
    D. It is decreasing as fast as everytime the value of x changes

    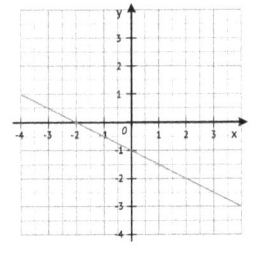

4. If a linear function is increasing...

    A. The value of y is increasing when the value of x is increasing
    B. The value of y is decreasing when the value of x is increasing
    C. The value of y is increasing for any value of x
    D. The value of y stays constant when the value of x is decreasing

5. The graph of which of the following functions has a minimum?

    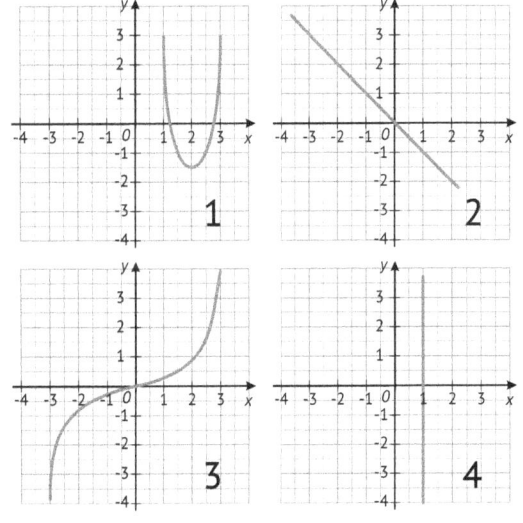

    A. 1   B. 2   C. 3   D. 4

TIP of the DAY

When doing the vertical line test, if a line intersects the graph at more than one point, then it is not a function.

WEEK 10 : DAY 3

1. How is the graph of a linear function changing with points (2, 8) and (6, 4)?

   A. It is constantly decreasing.
   B. It is constantly increasing.
   C. It is changing its direction.
   D. It is a horizontal line.

   8.F.B.5

2. The graph of which function is NOT decreasing and is NOT increasing?

   A. $y = 23 - 12x$
   B. $y = 3x^2$
   C. $y = x$
   D. $y = 3$

   8.F.B.5

3. The graph of which function is constantly decreasing?

   A. $y = 4 + 8x^3$
   B. $y = -6 + 10x$
   C. $y = \sqrt{x} + 6$
   D. $y = 18 - 3x$

   8.F.B.5

4. On what segment of the graph is the function decreasing?

   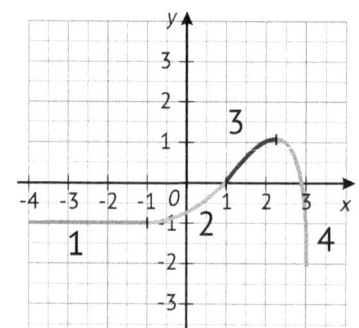

   A. 1
   B. 2
   C. 3
   D. 4

   8.F.B.5

5. Which of the following is a continuous function?

   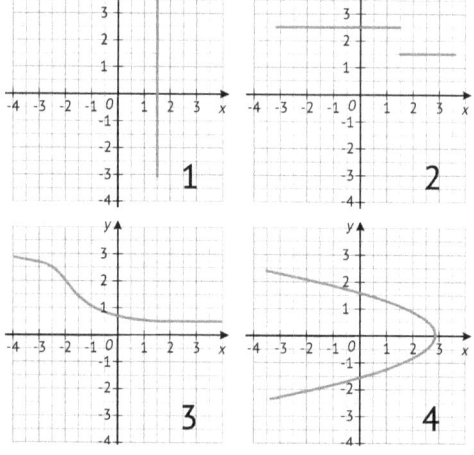

   Answer: _____

   8.F.B.5

The slope of a horizontal line is 0.

WEEK 10 : DAY 4

1. How is the graph of the function changing in the equation $y = 4 - x^2$?

   A. It is constantly decreasing.
   B. It is constantly increasing.
   C. It is changing its direction.
   D. It is a horizontal line.

   8.F.B.5

2. The graph of which of the following functions $y = 15 - 13x$ and $y = 4 - 10x$ is decreasing faster?

   A. $y = 15 - 13x$
   B. $y = 4 - 10x$
   C. Both are decreasing at the same rate.
   D. One is decreasing, and another one is increasing.

   8.F.B.5

3. The graph of which of the following functions has a maximum?

   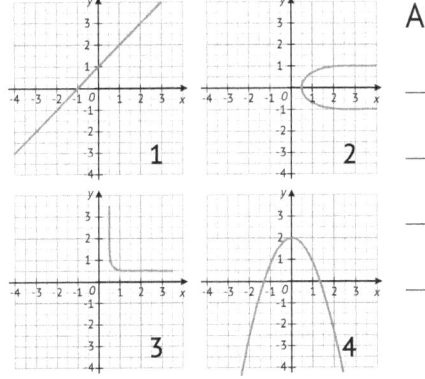

   Answer: _____
   _____
   _____
   _____
   _____

   8.F.B.5

4. The graph of which of the following functions $y = -10 + 18x$ and $y = 19x + 11$ is increasing faster?

   A. $y = -10 + 18x$
   B. $y = 19x + 11$
   C. Both are increasing at the same rate.
   D. One is decreasing, and another one is increasing

   8.F.B.5

5. If a linear function decreases...

   A. The value of y is increasing when the value of x is increasing
   B. The value of y is decreasing when the value of x is increasing
   C. The value of y is increasing for any value of x
   D. The value of y is decreasing when the value of x is decreasing

   8.F.B.5

6. Determine if the value of the function $y = -30 + x$ is decreasing or increasing if the value of x is increasing.

   Answer: _____

   8.F.B.5

TIP of the DAY

You should now be comfortable determining whether a function is increasing or decreasing and if it's a linear or nonlinear function.

69

WEEK 10 : DAY 5

ASSESSMENT

1. How is the graph of a linear function changing with points (5, 12) and (-1, 4)?

   A. It is constantly decreasing
   B. It is constantly increasing
   C. It is changing its direction
   D. It is a horizontal line

   8.F.B.5

2. The graph of which of the following functions $y = 21 + 12x$ and $y = 3x + 7$ is increasing faster?

   A. $y = 21 + 12x$
   B. $y = 3x + 7$
   C. Both are increasing at the same rate.
   D. One is decreasing, and another one is increasing.

   8.F.B.5

3. The graph of which of the following functions has a turning point?

   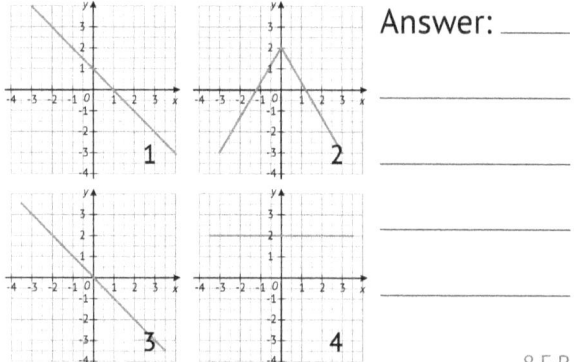

   Answer: _____
   _____
   _____
   _____

   8.F.B.5

4. The graph of which of the following functions $y = 18 + 6x$ and $y = -2x - 6$ is increasing faster?

   A. $y = 18 + 6x$
   B. $y = -2x - 6$
   C. Both are increasing at the same rate.
   D. One is decreasing, and another one is increasing.

   8.F.B.5

5. Does the function $y = 2x^2$ have a turning point?

   Answer: _____

   8.F.B.5

6. Which of the following functions has a minimum?

   A. $y = 15 + 1x$
   B. $y = 4$
   C. $y = -10x + 5$
   D. $y = 3x^2$

   8.F.B.5

DAY 6
Challenge question

Is a function constantly increasing or decreasing if it has the points (0, 4), (2, 7), (6, 10), and (8, 11)?

_____

8.F.B.5

70

WEEK 11

Week 11 is all about understanding rotations, reflections, and translations.

**You can find detailed video explanations of each problem in the book by visiting:
ArgoPrep.com/ccm8**

WEEK 11 : DAY 1

1. The line segment of 5 inches in length was translated to the right by 3 inches. Which statement is true?

   A. The line segment is now 8 inches in length
   B. The line segment is now 2 inches in length
   C. The length of the line segment has not changed.
   D. The line segment was divided into two line segments.

   8.G.A.1 & 8.G.A.2

2. After which operation does a horizontal line NOT coincide with the initial line?

   A. Rotation 180°
   B. Rotation 360°
   C. Reflection on the midpoint
   D. Translation upward by 10 inches

   8.G.A.1 & 8.G.A.2

3. How many degrees do you need to rotate an equilateral triangle relative to point *k* so that the rotated triangle coincides with the initial triangle?

   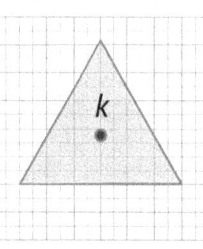

   A. 90°
   B. 120°
   C. 180°
   D. 270°

   8.G.A.1 & 8.G.A.2

4. An angle was rotated relative to its vertex. Which statement is true?

   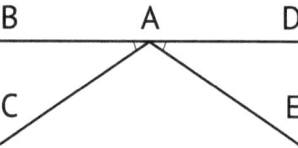

   A. ∠BAC = ∠DAE
   B. ∠BAC < ∠DAE
   C. ∠BAC > ∠DAE
   D. ∠BAC ≠ ∠DAE

   8.G.A.1 & 8.G.A.2

5. Which of the following operations - translation, rotation or reflection - should be applied to a line segment of 5 cm in length to turn it into a line segment of 10 cm in length?

   Answer: _____

   8.G.A.1 & 8.G.A.2

6. Which type of transformations - translation, rotation, or reflection - will separate the image from its preimage?

   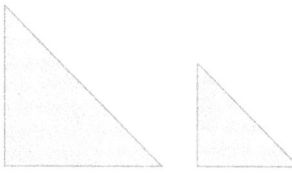

   Answer: _____

   8.G.A.1 & 8.G.A.2

Always double check your work!

WEEK 11 : DAY 2

1. A line was rotated 180°. Which statement is true?

   A. The rotated line is congruent to the initial line.
   B. The rotated line is crossing the initial line at an angle of 36°.
   C. The rotated line is perpendicular to the initial line.
   D. The rotated line is crossing the initial line at an angle of 75°.

   8.G.A.1 & 8.G.A.2

2. If an angle of 45° reflects relative to the vertex, the resulting angle will be of ...

   A. 45°   C. 120°
   B. 90°   D. 180°

   8.G.A.1 & 8.G.A.2

3. The square with a side of 3 inches was rotated 90° clockwise relative to vertex A. What will be the result?

   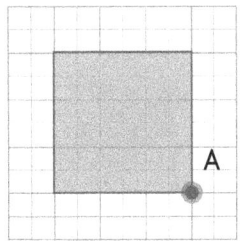

   A. It will double.
   B. It will translate to the right by 3 inches.
   C. It will translate down by 3 inches.
   D. It will turn into a triangle.

   8.G.A.1 & 8.G.A.2

4. Which statement does NOT allow us to draw a conclusion about the congruence of two triangles?

   A. The sides of one triangle are equal to the corresponding sides of another triangle.
   B. One triangle can be completely aligned with another triangle by rotation.
   C. Perimeters of both triangles are equal.
   D. The sum of the angles of both triangles is 180°.

   8.G.A.1 & 8.G.A.2

5. What will be the position of the two parallel straight lines if they are rotated 45° clockwise?

   Answer: _____

   8.G.A.1 & 8.G.A.2

6. What type of transformation occured?

   Answer: _____

   8.G.A.1 & 8.G.A.2

TIP of the DAY

A reflection is a transformation of the preimage that is flipped across a line of reflection to create the image.

WEEK 11 : DAY 3

1. An equilateral triangle was reflected relatively to the line passing through its side. What is the result?

   A. The second triangle has become bigger than the initial triangle.
   B. It turned into a versatile triangle.
   C. The second triangle has become smaller than the initial triangle.
   D. The second triangle is the same size as the initial triangle.

   8.G.A.1 & 8.G.A.2

2. Two horizontal lines are parallel. The distance between them is 10 cm. If one line will be translated down by 3 cm, what will happen to the lines?

   A. They will become perpendicular.
   B. They will cross each other.
   C. They will coincide.
   D. They will stay parallel.

   8.G.A.1 & 8.G.A.2

3. If an angle of 45° translates to the right by 10 cm, the new angle will be...

   A. 95°   C. 45°
   B. 105°   D. 35°

   8.G.A.1 & 8.G.A.2

4. Which of the following shapes is congruent to the shape shown below?

   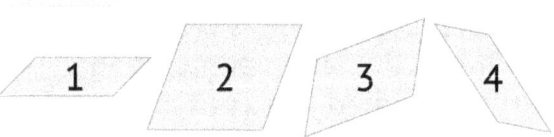

   A. 1   C. 3
   B. 2   D. 4

   8.G.A.1 & 8.G.A.2

5. How many degrees must an angle be rotated so that the ray of a new angle and the ray of the original angle lie on the same straight line?

   Answer: _____

   8.G.A.1 & 8.G.A.2

6. What transformation happens when you turn a page in a book?

   Answer: _____

   8.G.A.1 & 8.G.A.2

TIP of the DAY

When we dilate an image, we are changing the size of the figure. We can make it smaller or larger.

WEEK 11 : DAY 4

1. What transformation happened with line segment AB?

   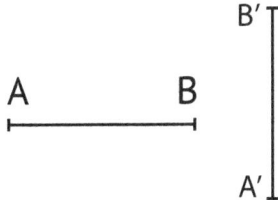

   A. It was translated by 3 cm.
   B. It was rotated 270° clockwise.
   C. It was reflected.
   D. It was rotated 90° clockwise.

   8.G.A.1 & 8.G.A.2

2. Two vertical parallel lines were reflected. What will happen to the lines after this transformation?

   A. They will stay parallel.
   B. Two lines will turn into one line.
   C. They will become longer.
   D. They will cross each other.

   8.G.A.1 & 8.G.A.2

3. Is it possible to enlarge an angle of 30° to 90° by rotation of 60° relative to its vertix?

   Answer: _____

   8.G.A.1 & 8.G.A.2

4. After rotation the line segment became congruent to the initial line segment. How many degrees was the line segment rotated?

   A. 45°
   B. 90°
   C. 120°
   D. 360°

   8.G.A.1 & 8.G.A.2

5. Determine which shapes are congruent?

   Answer: _____

   8.G.A.1 & 8.G.A.2

6. Two lines are parallel. They were rotated 90°. Which statement is true?

   A. The rotated lines are perpendicular.
   B. The rotated lines are congruent.
   C. They are parallel.
   D. The rotated lines are crossing each other.

   8.G.A.1 & 8.G.A.2

TIP of the DAY

Another type of transformation we are working with is rotation. When we rotate a figure, we are turning the figure around a fixed center point.

WEEK 11 : DAY 5

ASSESSMENT

1. $\triangle ABC \cong \triangle A'B'C'$. Which statement is FALSE?

   A. $\angle BAC < \angle B'A'C'$
   B. $\overline{AB} = \overline{A'B'}$
   C. $\angle ABC = \angle A'B'C'$
   D. $\overline{AB} + \overline{BC} = \overline{A'B'} + \overline{B'C'}$

   8.G.A.1 & 8.G.A.2

2. Are the two shapes shown below congruent?

   Answer: _____

   8.G.A.1 & 8.G.A.2

3. How many degrees should the shape be rotated clockwise to coincide with the original one?

   A. 45°
   B. 60°
   C. 100°
   D. 150°

   8.G.A.1 & 8.G.A.2

4. What transformation could a shape undergo so it remains congruent?

   A. Translation
   B. Rotation
   C. Reflection
   D. All of the above

   8.G.A.1 & 8.G.A.2

5. If the two shapes below are congruent, which statement is FALSE?

   A. $\angle BCD < \angle B'C'D'$
   B. $\overline{BC} = \overline{D'E'}$
   C. Line segment $B'D'$ is 10 cm in length
   D. $\triangle BCD \cong \triangle B'C'D'$

   8.G.A.1 & 8.G.A.2

6. If the square with a side of 6 cm is translated to the left by 3 cm, then the new shape will...

   A. Be twice as small than the initial shape.
   B. Turn into the parallelepiped with sides of 3 cm and 6 cm.
   C. Be equal to the initial shape.
   D. Turn into a parallelepiped with sides of 9 cm and 6 cm.

   8.G.A.1 & 8.G.A.2

DAY 6
Challenge question

Two vertical parallel lines are 5 cm apart. The right line was translated to the left by 2 cm, then both lines were rotated 270°. What is the position of the lines now on the coordinate plane and relative to each other?

_____

8.G.A.1 & 8.G.A.2

76

WEEK 12

In week 12 we will continue learning about the different types of transformations.

You can find detailed video explanations of each problem in the book by visiting: ArgoPrep.com/ccm8

WEEK 12 : DAY 1

1. Which of the following transformations will change the preimage into the image?

   preimage   image

   A. Translation
   B. Rotation
   C. Reflection
   D. Dilation

   8.G.A.3 & 8.G.A.4

2. Angle *ABC* and *EFG* are right angles on the quadrangles *ABCD* and *EFGH*. Which of the following statements is true?

   A. Both quadrangles are squares.
   B. Both quadrangles are rectangles.
   C. Both quadrangles are congruent.
   D. None of the above.

   8.G.A.3 & 8.G.A.4

3. The triangle with coordinates (1, 4), (4, 6), (2, 8) was reflected over the *y*-axis. What is one of the coordinates of the new triangle?

   A. (1, -4)   C. (-4, -6)
   B. (-2, 8)   D. (-1, -4)

   8.G.A.3 & 8.G.A.4

4. Two triangles are shown on the coordinate plane. Which statement is true?

   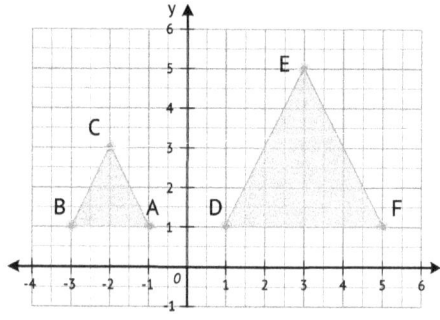

   A. $\overline{AB} = \overline{FD}$
   B. $\angle BAC = \angle DFE$
   C. $\angle BAC < \angle DFE$
   D. $\overline{AB} + \overline{BC} + \overline{CA} = \overline{FD} + \overline{DE} + \overline{EF}$

   8.G.A.3 & 8.G.A.4

5. Two triangles have the coordinates (-4, 1), (-2, 3), (-5, 4) and (2, -1), (0, -3), (3, -4). Are the two triangles similar or congruent?

   Answer: _____

   8.G.A.3 & 8.G.A.4

TIP of the DAY

Remember that congruent shapes have the same size and angle measurements.

78

WEEK 12 : DAY 2

1. Which statement is FALSE?

   A. Two congruent shapes are similar.
   B. If quadrangles have all equal angles, then they are congruent.
   C. The corresponding angles of similar triangles are equal.
   D. All squares are similar.

   8.G.A.3 & 8.G.A.4

2. Which of the following transformations will change the preimage into the image?

   preimage   image

   A. Reflection
   B. Translation and dilation
   C. Reflection and dilation
   D. Rotation and dilation

   8.G.A.3 & 8.G.A.4

3. Which transformation could change a trapezoid to a similar trapezoid but NOT congruent?

   A. Translation and rotation
   B. Rotation and dilation
   C. Translation and reflection
   D. Rotation and reflection

   8.G.A.3 & 8.G.A.4

4. $\triangle ABC$ was reflected over a vertical line and dilated by a factor of 2 relative to its center. The resulting image is $\triangle A'B'C'$. Which statement is FALSE?

   A. $\triangle ABC$ and $\triangle A'B'C'$ are similar.
   B. $\angle BAC = \angle B'A'C'$
   C. Perimeter of $\triangle A'B'C'$ is twice as big as the perimeter of $\triangle ABC$.
   D. The corresponding sides of these triangles are equal.

   8.G.A.3 & 8.G.A.4

5. What transformations do you have to do to turn $\triangle ABC$ into $\triangle DEF$?

   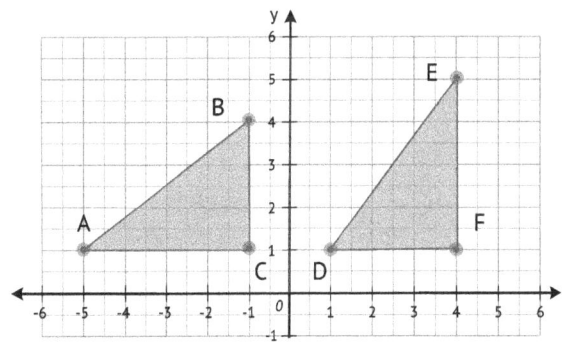

   Answer: _____

   8.G.A.3 & 8.G.A.4

TIP of the DAY

We can undergo a sequence of transformations to get to the new image. Pay attention if the shape got bigger or smaller. If so, that means we have dilated the preimage.

WEEK 12 : DAY 3

1. A trapezoid was reflected over its base and translated to the right. Which statement is true?

   A. The new trapezoid has become larger than the initial one.
   B. The new trapezoid is congruent to the initial one.
   C. The new trapezoid coincides with the initial one.
   D. The new shape is NOT a trapezoid.

   8.G.A.3 & 8.G.A.4

2. A square with coordinates (2, 2), (6, 2), (6, 6), (2, 6) was translated to the right by 5 units and upward by 3 units. What is one of the coordinates of the new square?

   A. (12, 9)   C. (11, 5)
   B. (5, 7)   D. (9, 7)

   8.G.A.3 & 8.G.A.4

3. Which of the following transformations will change the preimage into the image?

   preimage   image

   A. Rotation
   B. Rotation and dilation
   C. Dilation
   D. Translation and dilation

   8.G.A.3 & 8.G.A.4

4. The trapezoid with coordinates (1, -2), (2, 2), (4, 2), (5, -2) was reflected relative over the x-axis. Which point is one of the coordinates of the new trapezoid?

   A. (-1, 2)   C. (-4, 2)
   B. (2, -2)   D. (-5, 2)

   8.G.A.3 & 8.G.A.4

5. Write the coordinates of the shape shown in the picture.

   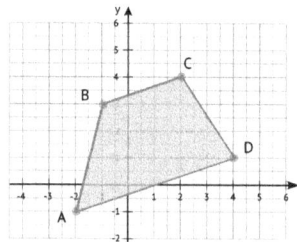

   Answer: _____

   8.G.A.3 & 8.G.A.4

6. Two triangles ABC and ADE are similar and they have the common point A with coordinates (3, 5). The triangle ADE is 3 times larger than the triangle ABC. What are the other two coordinates of triangle ADE, if the coordinates of vertex B are (4, 10) and the coordinates of vertex C are (6, 6)?

   Answer: _____

   8.G.A.3 & 8.G.A.4

TIP of the DAY

If you are given the coordinates of a preimage and image, it's always a good idea to graph it so you can visually see the transformation.

WEEK 12 : DAY 4

1. The circle with the center (-2, 5) was reflected relative to the center of the coordinates. What are the coordinates of the center of the new circle?

   A. (2, 5)
   B. (-5, 2)
   C. (-2, -5)
   D. (2, -5)

   8.G.A.3 & 8.G.A.4

2. The coordinates of △ABC are (2, 3), (2, 7), (5, 2). △ABC underwent a sequence of transformations and △A'B'C' had the coordinates (3, -1), (3, 3), (6, -2). What was the sequence of transformations?

   A. It was translated down by 2 units and to the right by 4 units.
   B. It was translated down by 1 unit and to the right by 4 units.
   C. It was translated down by 1 unit and to the left by 4 units.
   D. It was translated down by 4 units and to the right by 1 unit.

   8.G.A.3 & 8.G.A.4

3. The square with coordinates (-2, 2), (2, 2), (2, -2), (-2, -2) was rotated 90° clockwise and dilated by a factor of 2 relative to its center. What are the coordinates of the new square?

   Answer: _____

   8.G.A.3 & 8.G.A.4

4. Two parallelograms are shown on the coordinate plane. Which statement is true?

   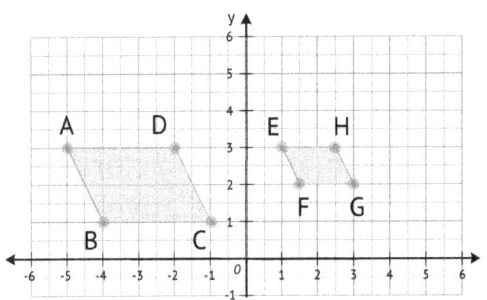

   A. $\overline{AB} = \overline{EF}$
   B. ∠BAD > ∠EHG
   C. The shapes are similar.
   D. The shapes are congruent.

   8.G.A.3 & 8.G.A.4

5. Which of the following transformations will change the preimage into the image?

   preimage   image

   A. Rotation and dilation
   B. Reflection and dilation
   C. Reflection, dilation, and rotation
   D. Reflection and rotation

   8.G.A.3 & 8.G.A.4

TIP of the DAY

Two shapes can be similar as long as the corresponding sides are proportional and corresponding angles are equal.

WEEK 12 : DAY 5

ASSESSMENT

1. The coordinates of the rectangle are (-2, -3), (4, -3), (-2, 1), (4, 1). After a transformation, the new coordinates were (-4, -3), (2, -3), (-4, 1), (2, 1). What was the transformation that occurred?

   A. It was dilated by a factor of 1.2.
   B. It was reflected relatively to axis y.
   C. It was translated to the left by 2 units.
   D. It was translated down by 2 units.

   8.G.A.3 & 8.G.A.4

2. In your own words, explain the difference between rotation, dilation and reflection.

   _____
   _____
   _____
   _____
   _____
   _____

   8.G.A.3 & 8.G.A.4

3. A circle with a radius of 4 units whose center lied at point (2, 3) was a dilated by a factor of 2 relative to its center and translated upward by 3 units. Which of the points lies on the circumference of the new circle?

   A. (13, 6)   C. (10, 6)
   B. (-6, 3)   D. (8, 3)

   8.G.A.3 & 8.G.A.4

4. Can two squares be congruent if one has a side with the coordinates (2, 2) and (2, 8), and the second square has a side with the coordinates (4, 3) and (5, 9)?

   Answer: _____

   8.G.A.3 & 8.G.A.4

5. The point with coordinates (2, -5) lies on the circumference. The center of this circumference has the coordinates (2, 1). Determine the radius of this circle.

   Answer: _____

   8.G.A.3 & 8.G.A.4

DAY 6
Challenge question

The triangle with the coordinates (-4, 1), (-1, 1), (-4, 4) was reflected relative to the line $y = -1$. Then the new triangle was reflected relative to the line $x = 1$. Write the coordinates of the third triangle.

_____

8.G.A.3 & 8.G.A.4

WEEK 13

In this week we will be learning about parallel lines that are cut by transversal lines and the special interior and exterior rules associated with that.

You can find detailed video explanations of each problem in the book by visiting:
ArgoPrep.com/ccm8

WEEK 13 : DAY 1

1. Below are two parallel lines with a third line intersecting them. Which statement is true?

   A. $m\angle 1 = m\angle 2$
   B. $m\angle 2 = m\angle 7$
   C. $m\angle 3 = m\angle 6$
   D. $m\angle 2 = m\angle 4$

   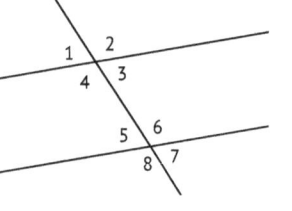

2. A triangle has sides of 4 cm, 4 cm and 5 cm in length. What kind of triangle is this?

   A. Right triangle
   B. Equilateral triangle
   C. Acute-angled triangle
   D. Obtuse triangle

3. Which statement is true?

   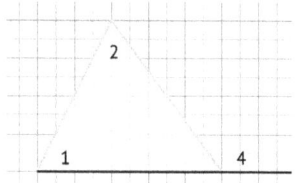

   A. $m\angle 4 = m\angle 1 + m\angle 2$
   B. $m\angle 2 = m\angle 4$
   C. $m\angle 2 + m\angle 3 = m\angle 4$
   D. $m\angle 3 = m\angle 4 - (m\angle 2 + m\angle 2)$

4. A triangle has sides of 6 cm, 5 cm and 8 cm in length. What kind of triangle is this?

   A. Right triangle
   B. Equilateral triangle
   C. Acute-angled triangle
   D. Obtuse triangle

5. The Pythagorean Theorem only works on what type of special triangles?

   Answer: _____

6. The exterior angle of the triangle is 60°. What is the value of the conjugated interior angle?

   Answer: _____

TIP of the DAY

A transversal line intersects two or more parallel lines. We will be working with a transversal line that intersects two parallel lines.

WEEK 13 : DAY 2

1. Below are two parallel lines with a third line intersecting them. Which statement is true?

   A. $m\angle 5 = m\angle 3$
   B. $m\angle 2 = m\angle 5$
   C. $m\angle 7 = m\angle 6$
   D. $m\angle 8 = m\angle 1$

   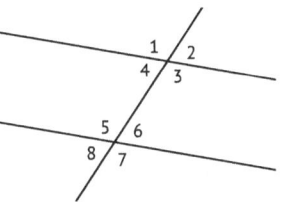

2. Which statement is true?

   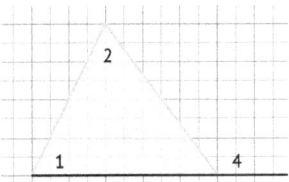

   A. $m\angle 1 + m\angle 2 = m\angle 4 - m\angle 3$
   B. $m\angle 1 + m\angle 3 = m\angle 4$
   C. $m\angle 4 + m\angle 2 = m\angle 1$
   D. $m\angle 3 = m\angle 4 - m\angle 1$

3. If the sides of the triangle are a = 2 cm, b = 4 cm, what is the area of the smaller square?

   A. 16 sq cm   C. 25 sq cm
   B. 20 sq cm   D. 36 sq cm

4. Which statement is true?

   A. All sides of a right triangle are equal.
   B. The square of one side of a right triangle is equal to the sum of the squares of the other two sides.
   C. The square of one side of a right triangle is equal to the square of the sum of the other two sides.
   D. The square of a hypotenuse of a right triangle is equal to the sum of the squares of the legs.

5. A triangle has one angle that measures 40° and another angle that measures 45°. How many degrees is the third angle?

   Answer: _____

6. Is it possible to apply the Pythagorean Theorem to an isosceles triangle?

   Answer: _____

TIP of the DAY

Since we have two lines that are cut by a transversal, we have to know a few rules. The pairs of consecutive interior angles that are formed are always supplementary (meaning both angles add up to 180°).

85

WEEK 13 : DAY 3

1. Below are three intersecting lines. Which statement is FALSE?

   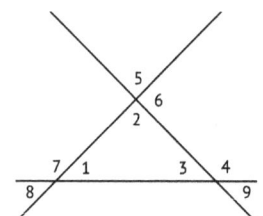

   A. $m\angle 4 + m\angle 3 = m\angle 4 + m\angle 9$
   B. $m\angle 4 + m\angle 3 = m\angle 3$
   C. $m\angle 9 + m\angle 1 + m\angle 2 = 180°$
   D. $m\angle 4 + m\angle 9 = m\angle 8 + m\angle 5 + m\angle 3$

   8.G.A.5 & 8.G.B.6

2. Which statement is FALSE?

   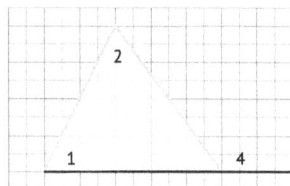

   A. $m\angle 2 + m\angle 3 = m\angle 4 - m\angle 1$
   B. $m\angle 1 + m\angle 2 = 180° - m\angle 3$
   C. $m\angle 4 + m\angle 3 = 180°$
   D. $m\angle 3 = 180° - m\angle 4$

   8.G.A.5 & 8.G.B.6

3. There are two parallel lines with the third line intersecting them. Which statement is FALSE?

   A. $m\angle 2 = m\angle 8$
   B. $m\angle 6 = m\angle 8$
   C. $m\angle 2 = m\angle 3$
   D. $m\angle 4 = m\angle 6$

   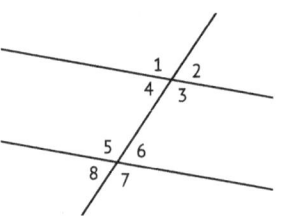

   8.G.A.5 & 8.G.B.6

4. Which of the following is true?

   A. $S_1^2 + S_2^2 = S_3^2$
   B. $S_1^2 + S_3^2 = S_2^2$
   C. $S_1^2 + S_3^2 > S_2^2$
   D. $S_1^2 + S_2^2 < S_3^2$

   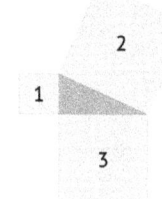

   8.G.A.5 & 8.G.B.6

5. Which theorem helps to identify a right triangle?

   Answer: _____

   8.G.A.5 & 8.G.B.6

6. Two of the angles in a triangle measure 45°. What kind of triangle is this?

   Answer: _____

   8.G.A.5 & 8.G.B.6

TIP of the DAY

An acute angle measures less than 90°.
An obtuse angle measures more than 90°.
A right angle measures 90°.

WEEK 13 : DAY 4

1. There are two parallel lines with the third line intersecting them. Which statement is true?

   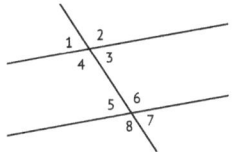

   A. All angles between the lines are equal.
   B. $m\angle 5 + m\angle 2 = m\angle 5 + m\angle 6$
   C. All angles have a different value.
   D. $m\angle 1 + m\angle 2 + m\angle 3 = m\angle 5 + m\angle 6 + m\angle 8$

   8.G.A.5 & 8.G.B.6

2. Using the picture given below, what could be proved?

   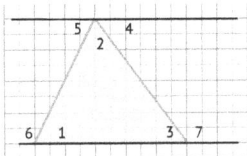

   A. The center of the circle inscribed in the triangle and the center of the circumference drawn around it coincide.
   B. The triangle is isosceles.
   C. The sum of the interior angles of the triangle is 180°.
   D. The interior angles of the triangle are always acute.

   8.G.A.5 & 8.G.B.6

3. A triangle has sides of 3 cm, 5 cm and 4 cm in length. What kind of this triangle is?

   A. Right triangle
   B. Equilateral triangle
   C. Acute-angled triangle
   D. Obtuse triangle

   8.G.A.5 & 8.G.B.6

4. A triangle has sides of 8 cm, 6 cm and 10 cm in length. Is this a right triangle?

   Answer: _____

   8.G.A.5 & 8.G.B.6

5. Angle 4 shown in the picture is 45°. Which statement is true?

   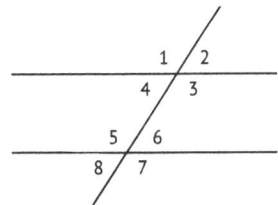

   A. $m\angle 1 + m\angle 2 + m\angle 3 = 320°$
   B. $m\angle 5 + m\angle 4 = 90°$
   C. $m\angle 7 + m\angle 5 = 270°$
   D. $m\angle 2 + m\angle 4 + m\angle 8 = 130°$

   8.G.A.5 & 8.G.B.6

TIP of the DAY

Angles on a straight line add to 180°.
Two angles are supplementary when they add up to 180°. In other words, two angles on a straight line are supplementary.

87

WEEK 13 : DAY 5

ASSESSMENT

1. Angle 3 shown in the picture is 60°. What is the measure of angle 8?

   A. 60°
   B. 90°
   C. 120°
   D. 180°

   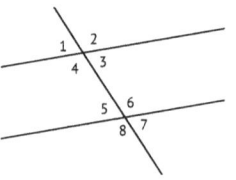

2. There are three intersecting lines. Which statement is true?

   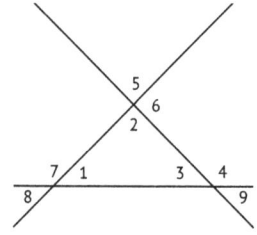

   A. $m\angle 3 = m\angle 4 = m\angle 9$
   B. $m\angle 5 = m\angle 3 = m\angle 7$
   C. $m\angle 6 + m\angle 5 + m\angle 9 = m\angle 4 + m\angle 9$
   D. $m\angle 7 = m\angle 3 + m\angle 2$

3. A triangle has sides of 5 cm, 7 cm and 8 cm in length. Is this a right triangle?

   Answer: _____

4. Which statement does NOT confirm that $ABC \cong ACD$?

   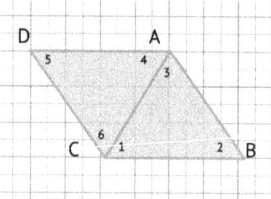

   A. $\overline{AB} = \overline{AD}, \overline{BC} = \overline{CD}, m\angle 2 = m\angle 5$
   B. $m\angle 2 = m\angle 5, m\angle 3 = m\angle 4, m\angle 1 = m\angle 6$
   C. $\overline{AB} = \overline{AD} \ \overline{BC} = \overline{CD}$
   D. $\overline{AB} = \overline{AD}, \overline{BC} = \overline{CD}, m\angle 4 = m\angle 3, m\angle 1 = m\angle 6$

5. There are two triangles with the corresponding angles of 50° and 70°. Are these triangles similar?

   Answer: _____

6. What is the sum of the interior angles of two triangles?

   Answer: _____

DAY 6
Challenge question

Two angles of a triangle measure 55° and 75°. Two angles of another triangle measure 75° and 50°. Are these two triangles similar?

_____

88

WEEK 14

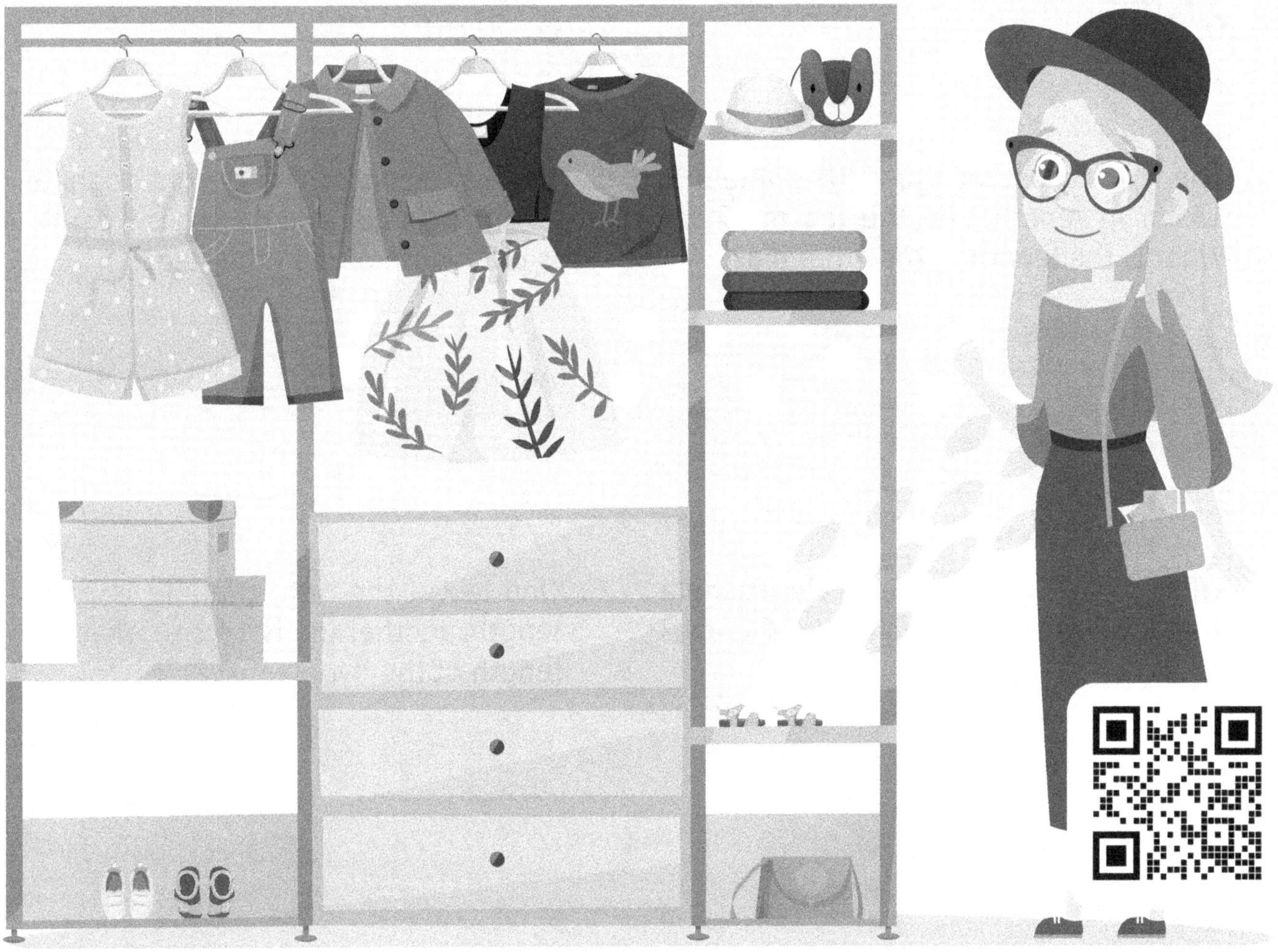

In week 14 we will be working with the Pythagorean Theorem to determine unknown side lengths in right triangles.

You can find detailed video explanations of each problem in the book by visiting:
ArgoPrep.com/ccm8

WEEK 14 : DAY 1

1. One leg of the right triangle is 3 cm in length, another leg is 4 cm. What is length of the hypotenuse?

   A. 5 cm
   B. 6 cm
   C. 8 cm
   D. 10 cm

2. The hypotenuse of the right triangle is 13 cm in length, and the leg is 12 cm. What is the length of the other leg?

   A. 4 cm
   B. 5 cm
   C. 6 cm
   D. 7 cm

3. What is the height of an isosceles triangle with a base of 30 cm and a side of 17 cm?

   A. 6 cm
   B. 8 cm
   C. 10 cm
   D. 12 cm

4. What is the hypotenuse of the right triangle if the legs measure 8 cm and 15 cm in length?

   A. 16 cm
   B. 17 cm
   C. 18 cm
   D. 20 cm

5. The hypotenuse of the right triangle is 15 cm in length, and the leg is 9 cm. What is the length of the other leg?

   Answer: _____

6. One leg of the right triangle is 7 cm in length, another leg is 14 cm. What is the length of the hypotenuse?

   Answer: _____

TIP of the DAY

In the Pythagorean formula, $a^2 + b^2 = c^2$, the value of c is the hypotenuse.

WEEK 14 : DAY 2

1. One leg of the right triangle is 9 cm in length, another leg is 12 cm. What is the length of the hypotenuse?

   A. 14 cm
   B. 15 cm
   C. 16 cm
   D. 18 cm

2. Which of the following is a Pythagorean Triple?

   A. 3 - 4 - 6
   B. 14 - 18 - 20
   C. $9 - 9 - 9\sqrt{2}$
   D. $7 - 8 - 8\sqrt{3}$

3. What is the hypotenuse of the right triangle with legs of 35 cm and 84 cm in length?

   A. 89 cm
   B. 91 cm
   C. 96 cm
   D. 100 cm

4. The hypotenuse of the right triangle is 10 cm in length, and the leg is 6 cm. What is the length of the other leg?

   A. 5 cm
   B. 6 cm
   C. 7 cm
   D. 8 cm

5. Thomas bought a painting that measures 45 inches by 28 inches. He has a frame that can fit a 50-inch-diagonal painting. Will this frame fit the picture? Explain why or why not.

   Answer: _____

6. Mary is building a slide. If the ladder is 6 feet tall and she wants the bottom of the slide to be 8 feet from the ladder, how long does the slide need to be?

   Answer: _____

Please note you can only apply the Pythagorean Theorem to triangles with a right angle.

WEEK 14 : DAY 3

1. Which of the following is a Pythagorean Triple?

   A. 6 - 8 - 9√2
   B. 12 - 14 - 15
   C. 3 - 6 - 8
   D. √3 - √5 - √8

2. What is the hypotenuse of the right triangle with both legs measuring 1 cm in length?

   A. 1 cm
   B. 2 cm
   C. √2 cm
   D. √3 cm

3. What is the height of a rectangle with a diagonal measuring 25 cm and a base measuring 24 cm?

   A. 5 cm
   B. 6 cm
   C. 7 cm
   D. 8 cm

4. One leg of the right triangle is 5 cm in length, another leg is 5 cm. What is the length of the hypotenuse?

   A. 6 cm
   B. 3√3 cm
   C. 7 cm
   D. 5√2 cm

5. A football field is a rectangle that measures 90 meters wide and 120 meters long. If a player runs from one corner to the corner diagonally across the field, what is the distance the player will run?

   Answer: _____

6. What is the length of the diagonal of a 12 cm by 20 cm rectangle?

   Answer: _____

Remember that a rectangle has four right angles. If we take a look at a diagonal of a rectangle, that would be the hypotenuse of one of the triangles.

WEEK 14 : DAY 4

1. The hypotenuse of the right triangle is 25 cm in length, and the leg is 15 cm. What is the length of the other leg?

   A. 18 cm
   B. 20 cm
   C. 22 cm
   D. 24 cm

2. If the diagonal of a square is 42 cm, what is the length of one of its sides?

   A. $21 \times \sqrt{2}$ cm
   B. $21 \times \sqrt{3}$ cm
   C. $21 \times \sqrt{4}$ cm
   D. 40 cm

3. Find the length of the diagonal of a rectangle that has a length of 12 cm and a width of 9 cm.

   A. 15 cm
   B. 16 cm
   C. 17 cm
   D. 18 cm

4. What is the hypotenuse of the right triangle with legs of 12 cm and 15 cm in length?

   A. $3\sqrt{41}$ cm
   B. 14 cm
   C. $4\sqrt{13}$ cm
   D. 16 cm

5. Take a look at the diagram below. What is the measure of the unknown side?

   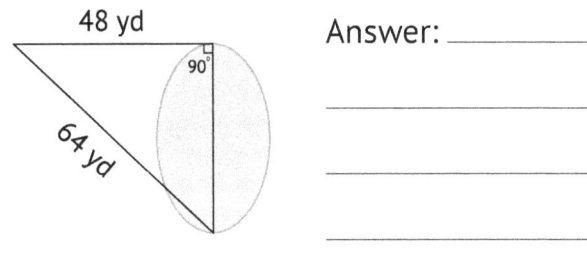

   Answer: _____

6. Lisa rides her bike 14 km north and then 9 km west. How far is she from her starting point?

   Answer: _____

Always draw a picture when working with word problems to help you determine the correct setup to avoid simple errors.

WEEK 14 : DAY 5

ASSESSMENT

1. The perimeter of a rectangle is 56 cm. The point of intersection of the diagonals is 6 cm from one of its sides. Find the length of the diagonal.

   A. 18 cm
   B. 20 cm
   C. 24 cm
   D. 28 cm

   8.G.B.7

2. The hypotenuse of a right triangle is 12 cm in length and the leg is 8 cm. What is the length of the second leg?

   A. 4 cm
   B. $4\sqrt{2}$ cm
   C. $4\sqrt{5}$ cm
   D. 5 cm

   8.G.B.7

3. Find the diagonal of the square with a perimeter of 36 cm.

   A. 10 cm
   B. $8\sqrt{4}$ cm
   C. 12 cm
   D. $9\sqrt{2}$ cm

   8.G.B.7

4. What is the length of a side of a rhombus with the diagonals of 24 cm and 32 cm?

   A. 16 cm
   B. 18 cm
   C. 20 cm
   D. 22 cm

   8.G.B.7

5. Julie has a square box with a side measuring 8 inches. Can Julie put this box into a round casket if its diameter is 10 inches?

   Answer: _____

   8.G.B.7

6. Joe rides his motorcycle 9 km south and then 12 km east. How far is he from his starting point?

   Answer: _____

   8.G.B.7

DAY 6
Challenge question

A football field is a rectangle that measures 50 meters wide and 120 meters long. If a player runs from one corner to the corner diagonally across the field, what is the distance the player will run?

_____

8.G.B.7

94

Let's practice finding the distance between two points in a coordinate system using the Pythagorean theorem.

You can find detailed video explanations of each problem in the book by visiting: ArgoPrep.com/ccm8

WEEK 15 : DAY 1

1. What is the distance between the points (-3, 1) and (9, 10)?

    A. 14
    B. 15
    C. 16
    D. 17

2. What are the coordinates of two points if the distance between them is 50 units?

    A. (22, -20) and (-18, 10)
    B. (26, 32) and (10, 11)
    C. (4, -6) and (45, -36)
    D. (0, 50) and (3, 56)

3. The distance between the point (5, 3) and another point is 13. What are the coordinates of this other point?

    A. (8, 6)   C. (6, 15)
    B. (10, 5)   D. (10, 15)

4. The hypotenuse of the right triangle lies between the points (-6, -1) and (-3, 3). What of the following are the coordinates of the third point if one of the legs is 4 units long?

    A. (-6, 2)   C. (-1, -6)
    B. (-3, -1)   D. (3, -2)

5. What is the length of the line segment?

    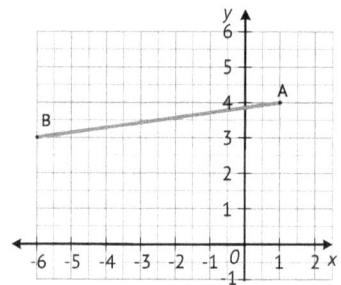

    Answer: _____

6. What is the distance between the points (-5, 4) and (4, -8)?

    Answer: _____

TIP of the DAY

We can find the length of a line segment on a coordinate graph using the Pythagorean Theorem by drawing the two legs and applying the formula.

WEEK 15 : DAY 2

1. What is the distance between the points (2, 2) and (6, 5)?

   A. 3
   B. 4
   C. 5
   D. 6

   8.G.B.8

2. The distance between the point (-2, 1) and another point is 20. What are the coordinates of the other point?

   A. (10, 17)
   B. (10, 15)
   C. (8, 18)
   D. (12, 12)

   8.G.B.8

3. What are the coordinates of two points if the distance between them is 26 units?

   A. (4, -15) and (-5, 20)
   B. (3, -8) and (-7, 16)
   C. (5, -8) and (11, 13)
   D. (-4, 10) and (6, 16)

   8.G.B.8

4. Which of the following points can be the vertices of a right triangle?

   A. (5, 6), (10, 8), (11, 6)
   B. (4, 4), (4, 6), (10, 6)
   C. (-2, 3), (2, 4), (0, 16)
   D. (8, 14), (14, 8), (11, 9)

   8.G.B.8

5. What is the distance between the two points?

   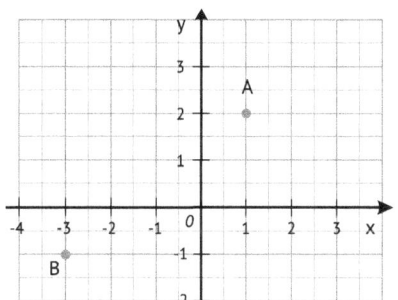

   Answer: _____

   8.G.B.8

6. Using the Pythagorean Theorem, find the distance between the points (20, 33) and (-15, -51).

   Answer: _____

   8.G.B.8

TIP of the DAY

A right triangle means one of the angles is 90° and the Pythagorean Theorem can be applied.

97

WEEK 15 : DAY 3

1. What is the distance between the points (-1, 1) and (7, 7)?

   A. 10
   B. 11
   C. 12
   D. 13

2. The distance between the point (6, 6) and another point is 26. What are the coordinates of the other point?

   A. (22, 22)
   B. (-10, -12)
   C. (-18, 16)
   D. (14, 26)

3. What are the coordinates of two points if the distance between them is 15 units?

   A. (-12, 4) and (-3, -8)
   B. (6, 7) and (12, 17)
   C. (2, -6) and (-10, 10)
   D. (-1, 16) and (7, 28)

4. Which of the following points can be the vertices of a right triangle?

   A. (3, 7), (8, 8), (4, 9)
   B. (2, 2), (4, 4), (5, 8)
   C. (-4, 1), (3, 5), (1, 10)
   D. (0, 2), (12, 7), (12, 2)

5. What is the distance between the two points?

   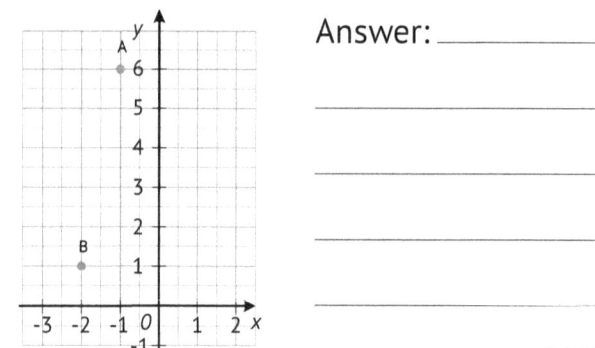

   Answer: _____

6. Using the Pythagorean Theorem, find the distance between the points (8, 3) and (-1, -6).

   Answer: _____

TIP of the DAY

Always double check your math work especially when working with formulas such as the Pythagorean Theorem or the distance formula.

98

WEEK 15 : DAY 4

1. What is the distance between the points (-4, 3) and (8, 8)?

   A. 10
   B. 11
   C. 12
   D. 13

   8.G.B.8

2. What are the coordinates of two points if the distance between them is 25 units?

   A. (-10, 16) and (8, 21)
   B. (-8, 9) and (16, 4)
   C. (2, 7) and (18, 12)
   D. (-15, 8) and (9, 1)

   8.G.B.8

3. Which of the following points can be the vertices of a right triangle?

   A. (-2, 0), (1, 0), (-2, 10)
   B. (5, 6), (7, 5), (9, 8)
   C. (0, 1), (0, 5), (3, 8)
   D. (3, -3), (4, -5), (5, 2)

   8.G.B.8

4. The hypotenuse of a right triangle lies between the points (-6, 5) and (2, -1). Which of the following is the coordinates of the third point if one of the legs is 6 units long?

   A. (2, -2)   C. (1, -2)
   B. (-1, -2)   D. (2, 5)

   8.G.B.8

5. What is the length of the line segment?

   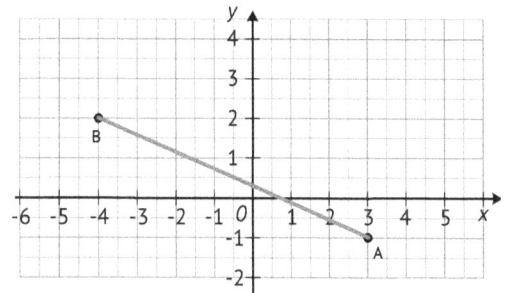

   Answer: _____

   8.G.B.8

6. Find the distance between the points (8, -27) and (4, -31).

   Answer: _____

   8.G.B.8

Did you know the hypotenuse is the longest side of a triangle?

WEEK 15 : DAY 5

ASSESSMENT

1. The distance between the point (-5, -2) and another point is 53. What are the coordinates of the other point?

   A. (19, 36)
   B. (23, 43)
   C. (-23, -14)
   D. (-21, -16)

2. Find the distance between the points (-4, 10) and (16, -5).

   A. 20
   B. 23
   C. 25
   D. 27

3. Find the distance between the points (-6, -2) and (9, 6).

   A. 16
   B. 17
   C. 18
   D. 19

4. What are the coordinates of two points if the distance between them is 13 units?

   A. (-3, 7) and (12, 5)
   B. (6, 12) and (8, 15)
   C. (10, -4) and (5, 8)
   D. (-1, 0) and (12, 14)

5. Find the distance between the points (11, -19) and (3, -4).

   Answer: _____

6. What is the distance between the points (-6, 9) and (42, 73)?

   Answer: _____

DAY 6
Challenge question

Find the length of the hypotenuse of the right triangle with the vertices at the points (2, 4), (-8, 4), (-8, -20).

100

WEEK 16

In week 16 we will work with word problems that deal with understanding volume formulas for cones, cylinders, and spheres. Make sure you know all the formulas!

**You can find detailed video explanations of each problem in the book by visiting:
ArgoPrep.com/ccm8**

WEEK 16 : DAY 1

1. What is the volume of a cone with a radius of 10 cm and a height of 15 cm?

   A. 450π cm^3
   B. 500π cm^3
   C. 550π cm^3
   D. 600π cm^3

   8.G.C.9

2. Find the height of a cone if its volume is 135π cm^3 and its radius is 9 cm.

   A. 4 cm
   B. 5 cm
   C. 6 cm
   D. 7 cm

   8.G.C.9

3. The volume of a cone is 245π cm^3. Find the height and the radius of this cone.

   A. $r = 7$ cm, $h = 15$ cm
   B. $r = 15$ cm, $h = 10$ cm
   C. $r = 12$ cm, $h = 16$ cm
   D. $r = 16$ cm, $h = 12$ cm

   8.G.C.9

4. What is the height and radius of a cylinder if the volume is $2,025\pi$ cm^3?

   A. $r = 8$ cm, $h = 20$ cm
   B. $r = 14$ cm, $h = 15$ cm
   C. $r = 9$ cm, $h = 25$ cm
   D. $r = 6$ cm, $h = 24$ cm

   8.G.C.9

5. Mr. Brown wants to place a water heater that has a volume of 100 liters and a diameter of 40 cm into a strong-box. Will the water heater fit in the strong-box if it has a width of 45 cm and a height of 90 cm? Use π as 3.14.

   Answer: _____

   8.G.C.9

6. A spherical vessel with a radius of 6 meters needs to pour its liquid into cylindrical vessels that each have a radius of 6 meters and a height of 4 meters. How many cylindrical vessels are needed? Use π as 3.14.

   Answer: _____

   8.G.C.9

Remember the volume formula for a cylinder:
$V = \pi \times r^2 \times h$

WEEK 16 : DAY 2

1. Find the volume of a cone if it is 5 cm in height and its radius is 3 cm.

   A. 15π cm³
   B. 16π cm³
   C. 180π cm³
   D. 20π cm³

   8.G.C.9

2. What is the volume of a cylinder with a radius of 4 cm and a height of 6 cm?

   A. 92π cm³
   B. 88π cm³
   C. 96π cm³
   D. 76π cm³

   8.G.C.9

3. What is the radius of a sphere with a volume of $4,500\pi$ cm³?

   A. 10 cm
   B. 15 cm
   C. 18 cm
   D. 20 cm

   8.G.C.9

4. What is the height of a cylinder if its volume is $1,200\pi$ cm³ and the radius is 10 cm?

   A. 10 cm   C. 12 cm
   B. 11 cm   D. 13 cm

   8.G.C.9

5. The Smiths reserve water in a barrel that has a diameter of 10 inches and a height of 50 inches. The Morgans reserve water in a barrel that has a diameter of 12 inches and a height of 40 inches. Which family is able to reserve more water in the barrel? Use π as 3.14.

   Answer: _____

   8.G.C.9

6. Christie wants to pour the juice from a cylindrical glass that has a diameter of 4 cm into a glass that is in the form of a cone with a diameter of 8 cm and a height of 3 cm. Will the juice fit into the conical glass if the height of the juice in the cylindrical glass measures 4 cm? Use π as 3.14.

   Answer: _____

   8.G.C.9

TIP of the DAY

Remember the volume formula for a sphere:
$V = \frac{4}{3} \times \pi \times r^3$

WEEK 16 : DAY 3

1. Find the radius of a cone if its volume is 168π cm^3 and its height is 14 cm.

   A. 10 cm
   B. 8 cm
   C. 7 cm
   D. 6 cm

   8.G.C.9

2. The volume of a cylinder is 882π cm^3. Find its height and radius.

   A. $r = 7$ cm, $h = 18$ cm
   B. $r = 10$ cm, $h = 16$ cm
   C. $r = 15$ cm, $h = 8$ cm
   D. $r = 12$ cm, $h = 14$ cm

   8.G.C.9

3. Find the volume of a sphere that has a radius of 6 cm.

   A. 329π cm^3
   B. 256π cm^3
   C. 368π cm^3
   D. 288π cm^3

   8.G.C.9

4. What is the radius of a sphere if it has a volume of 972π cm^3?

   A. 6 cm
   B. 7 cm
   C. 8 cm
   D. 9 cm

   8.G.C.9

A cylindrical container that has a height of 20 cm and a diameter of 12 cm was filled with perfume. Part of the perfume was poured into 10 spherical bottles that each had a diameter of 6 cm. **Use the information above to answer questions 5-6.**

5. How much perfume is left in the container? Use π as 3.14.

   Answer: _____

   8.G.C.9

6. Roughly, how many spherical bottles are needed to pour the entire volume of the perfume?

   Answer: _____

   8.G.C.9

Remember the volume formula for a cone:
$V = \pi \times r^2 \times \dfrac{h}{3}$

WEEK 16 : DAY 4

1. Find the height of a cone if its volume is 384π cm³ and the radius is 12 cm.

    A. 5 cm
    B. 6 cm
    C. 7 cm
    D. 8 cm

2. What is the height of a cylinder if its volume is 576π cm³ and its radius is 6 cm?

    A. 14 cm
    B. 16 cm
    C. 18 cm
    D. 20 cm

3. What is the volume of a sphere with a radius of 12 cm?

    A. 2,304π cm³
    B. 1,986π cm³
    C. 986π cm³
    D. 1,368π cm³

4. What is the diameter of a sphere that has a volume of 36π cm³?

    A. 6 cm
    B. 8 cm
    C. 10 cm
    D. 12 cm

5. Julia needs to measure 500 milliliters of juice to make a drink. She uses a glass that has a diameter of 4 cm and a height of 10 cm. How many glasses of juice should Julia take to make the drink? Use π as 3.14.

    Answer: _____

6. There is an aquarium in the form of a sphere that has a radius of 15 inches. How much water do you need to fill the aquarium completely? Use π as 3.14.

    Answer: _____

For these problems, you should be using a calculator. On the state exam, you will be permitted to use a scientific calculator.

WEEK 16 : DAY 5

ASSESSMENT

1. Find the volume of a cylinder with a radius of 11 cm and a height of 8 cm.

   A. 923π cm^3
   B. 798π cm^3
   C. 986π cm^3
   D. 968π cm^3

   8.G.C.9

2. Find the radius of a cylinder if its volume is 500π cm^3 and its height is 20 cm.

   A. 4 cm
   B. 5 cm
   C. 6 cm
   D. 8 cm

   8.G.C.9

3. Find the volume of a sphere with a radius of 15 cm.

   A. $3,129\pi$ cm^3
   B. $2,978\pi$ cm^3
   C. $4,500\pi$ cm^3
   D. $3,896\pi$ cm^3

   8.G.C.9

4. What is the radius of a cone if its volume is 168π cm^3 and its height is 14 cm?

   A. 4 cm
   B. 5 cm
   C. 6 cm
   D. 8 cm

   8.G.C.9

There are 2,500 milliliters of ice cream that must be packed in portions.

5. How many balls of ice-cream can be made if the diameter of one such ball is 5 cm? Use π as 3.14. Round your answer to the nearest whole number.

   Answer: _____

   8.G.C.9

DAY 6
Challenge question

Which of the following shapes has the largest volume: a cone with a radius of 7 cm and height of 8 cm, a cylinder with a radius of 4 cm and height of 6 cm or a sphere with a radius of 5 cm?

_____

8.G.C.9

106

WEEK 17

VIDEO EXPLANATIONS

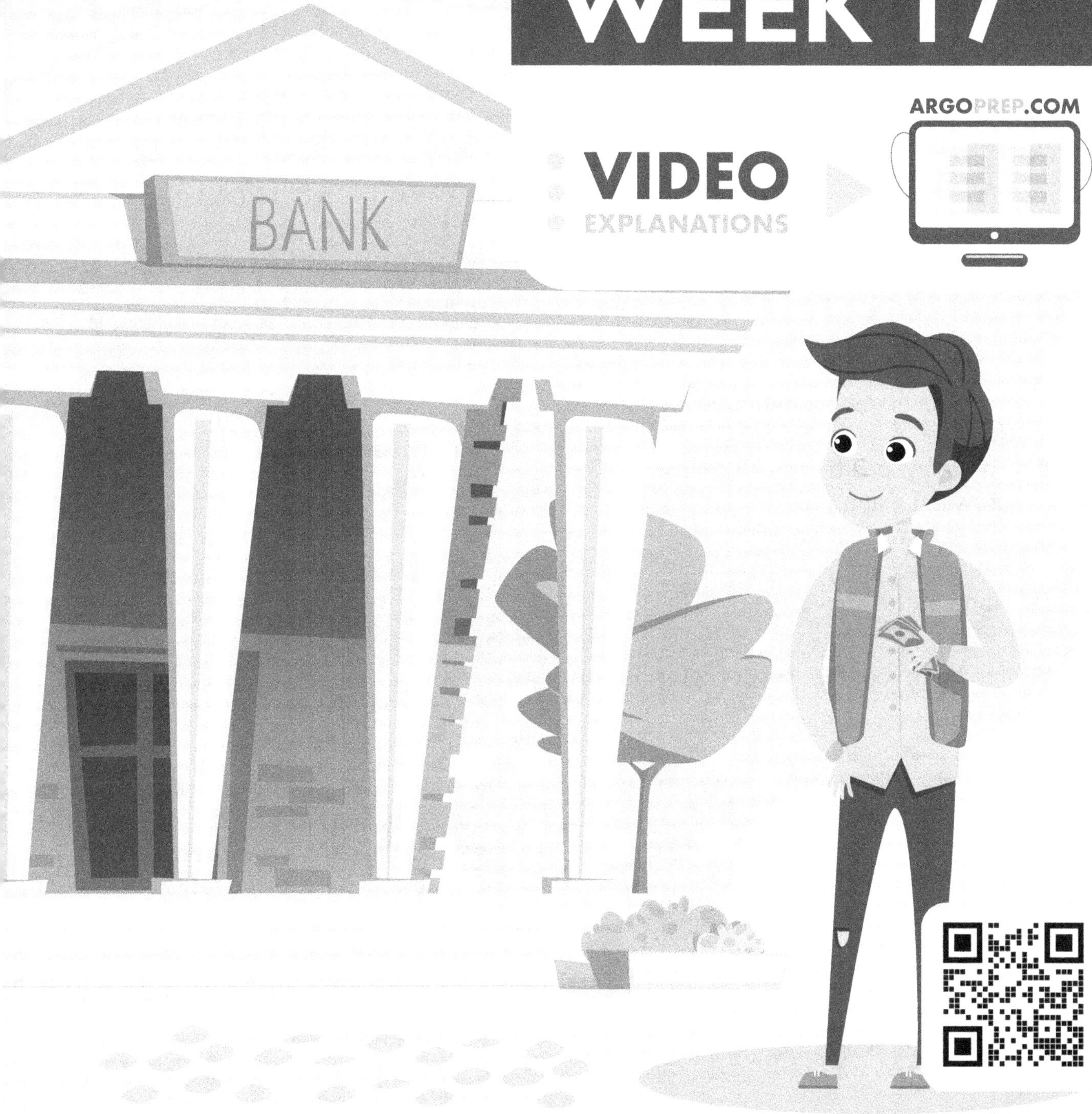

Did someone say scatter plots? Oh yeah! This week is all about learning to interpret scatter plots and determine patterns such as clustering, outliers, positive or negative association, linear association, and nonlinear association.

You can find detailed video explanations of each problem in the book by visiting:
ArgoPrep.com/ccm8

WEEK 17 : DAY 1

1. Which statement is true?

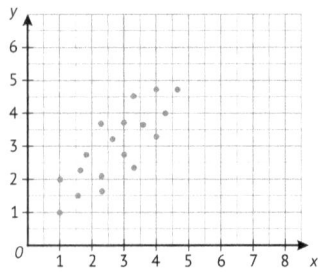

   A. There is no association between x and y.
   B. There is a positive association between x and y.
   C. There is a negative association between x and y.
   D. None of the above.

   8.G.C.9

2. Which point on the scatter plot is an outlier?

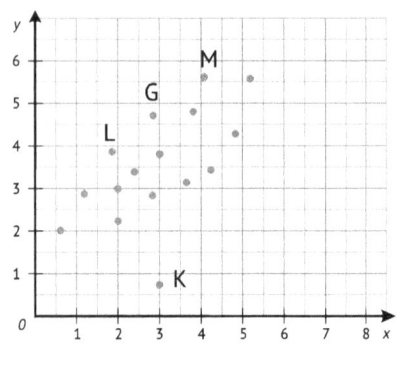

   A. G   B. K   C. L   D. M

   8.G.C.9

Data about the age and the average quantity of visitors at the movies per day are shown in the chart. **Solve questions 3-4, using the data below.**

The age of visitors (years old)	14	15	16	17	18	19	20	21
The average quantity of visitors per day	620	600	620	580	560	500	400	380

3. Using the data given in the chart, construct a scatter plot.

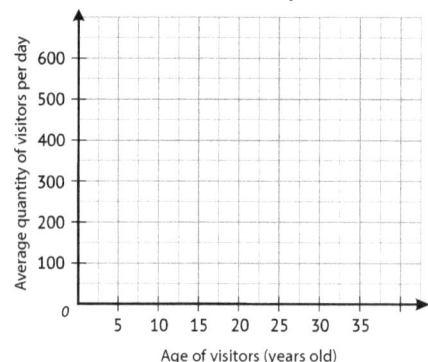

   8.G.C.9

4. Using the scatter plot above, what association can be seen between the age of visitors and the average quantity of visitors per day?

   A. Positive association
   B. Negative association
   C. Clustering
   D. Nonlinear association

   8.G.C.9

TIP of the DAY

A positive association or correlation is when one variable increases and the other one also increases.

WEEK 17 : DAY 2

1. Which statement is true?

   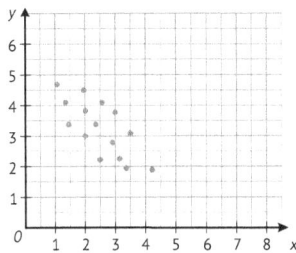

   A. There is no association between x and y.
   B. There is a positive association between x and y.
   C. There is a negative association between x and y.
   D. None of the above.

   8.G.C.9

The data in the chart below shows the association between study time (in months) of Spanish and the average quantity of new words learned.

Study time (months)	1	2	3	4	5	6	7	8
Average quantity of words learned	50	110	135	200	260	305	370	440

2. Which scatter plot on the top right shows the data correctly?

   A. 1
   B. 2
   C. 3
   D. 4

   8.G.C.9

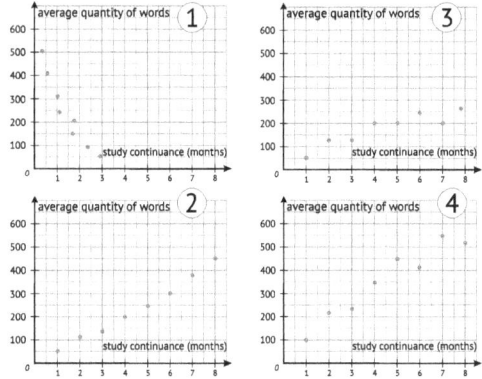

3. Which type of scatter plot would suggest a positive association?

   A. If one variable is increasing, another variable is decreasing.
   B. If one variable is decreasing, another variable is increasing.
   C. If one variable is increasing, then another variable is increasing, too.
   D. None of the above

   8.G.C.9

4. Which of the following does NOT correspond to a positive association?

   A. The time of building and the height of the walls of the building.
   B. The length of a pencil and the duration of using it.
   C. The age of teenagers and their average height.
   D. The average quantity of pencils used by schoolchildren and the duration of their study.

   8.G.C.9

TIP of the DAY

Negative association is when one of the values of the variable decreases and the other value increases.

WEEK 17 : DAY 3

1. Which statement is true?

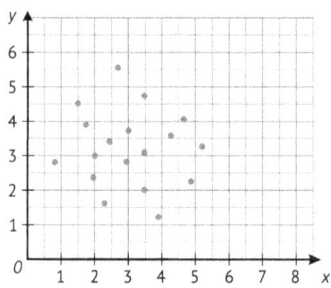

   A. There is no association between x and y.
   B. There is a positive association between x and y.
   C. There is a negative association between x and y.
   D. None of the above.

   8.G.C.9

2. What would be an example of a negative association?

   A. The more hours you ride a bicycle, the more calories burned.
   B. A decrease of air temperature in autumn results in fewer leaves on the trees.
   C. Increasing the power of computers reduces the time required for calculations.
   D. Increasing the power of computers increases the number of computing operations performed per unit time.

   8.G.C.9

Use the following scatter plots to answer questions 3-6.

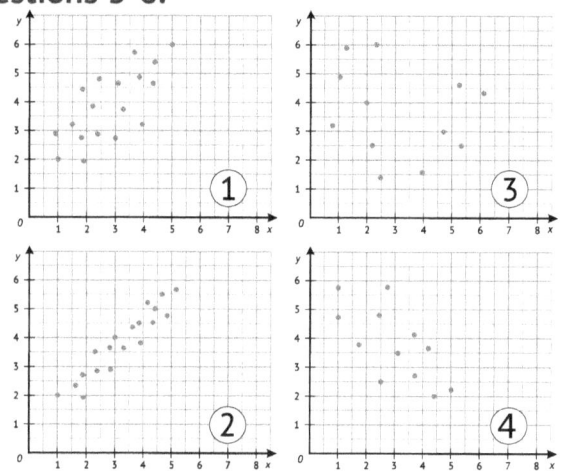

3. Which scatter plot shows the strongest correlation between the data? 8.G.C.9
   A. 1   B. 2   C. 3   D. 4

4. Which scatter plot shows the weakest correlation between the data? 8.G.C.9
   A. 1   B. 2   C. 3   D. 4

5. Which scatter plot shows a negative association between the data? 8.G.C.9
   A. 1   B. 2   C. 3   D. 4

6. Which scatter plot shows no association between x and y? 8.G.C.9
   A. 1   B. 2   C. 3   D. 4

Tip of the Day: When a data value does not fit the general trend of data, it is called an outlier.

WEEK 17 : DAY 4

1. Which situation would suggest a negative association in a scatter plot?

   A. If one variable is increasing, another variable is decreasing.
   B. If one variable is decreasing, then another variable is decreasing, too.
   C. If one variable is increasing, then another variable is increasing, too.
   D. None of the above.

   8.G.C.9

2. How many clusters can be distinguished in the scatter plot given below?

   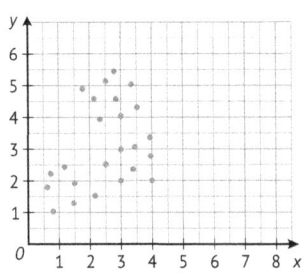

   A. 1
   B. 2
   C. 3
   D. None of the above

   8.G.C.9

3. Which dot is an outlier?

   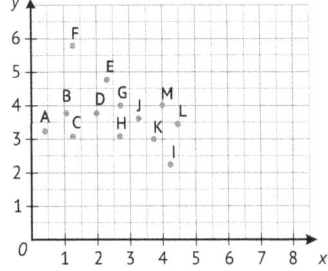

   Answer: _____

   8.G.C.9

The chart shows the data on how the amount of $1000 invested in a bank changed over a decade. **Using the data below, answer questions 4 - 5.**

period (year)	1	2	3	4	5	6	7	8	9	10
The value of the deposit at the end of the period ($)	1,050	1,103	1,158	1,216	1,276	1,340	1,407	1,477	1,551	1,628

4. Construct a scatter plot.

   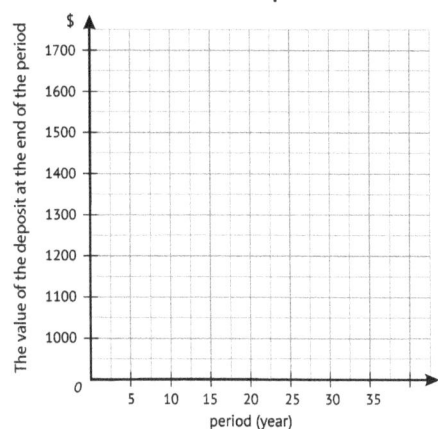

   8.G.C.9

5. Using the scatter plot above, what association can be seen between the period of deposit and the value of the deposit at the end of the period?

   A. Positive association
   B. Negative association
   C. Clustering
   D. Nonlinear association

   8.G.C.9

TIP of the DAY

If points are clustered and following the trend line, a strong association exists. If points do not lie generally on the trend line, the association is weaker. Learn to identify strong and weak associations.

111

WEEK 17 : DAY 5

ASSESSMENT

1. Which would be an example of a positive association?

   A. Increasing the air temperature and reducing the amount of Arctic ice.
   B. Increasing age of a tree and increasing its height.
   C. Increasing the prices for goods and reducing consumption of them.
   D. Increasing the duration of language learning and reducing the number of mistakes.

   8.G.C.9

2. Which scatter plot shows a negative association?

   A. 1
   B. 2
   C. 3
   D. 4

   8.G.C.9

3. Which scatter plot shows a nonlinear association?

   A. 1
   B. 2
   C. 3
   D. 4

   8.G.C.9

4. Which scatter plot could be described as clustering?

   A. 1
   B. 2
   C. 3
   D. 4

   8.G.C.9

5. Which scatter plot is characterized by the weakest correlation between the data?

   A. 1
   B. 2
   C. 3
   D. 4

   8.G.C.9

Use the following scatter plots below to answer questions 2-5.

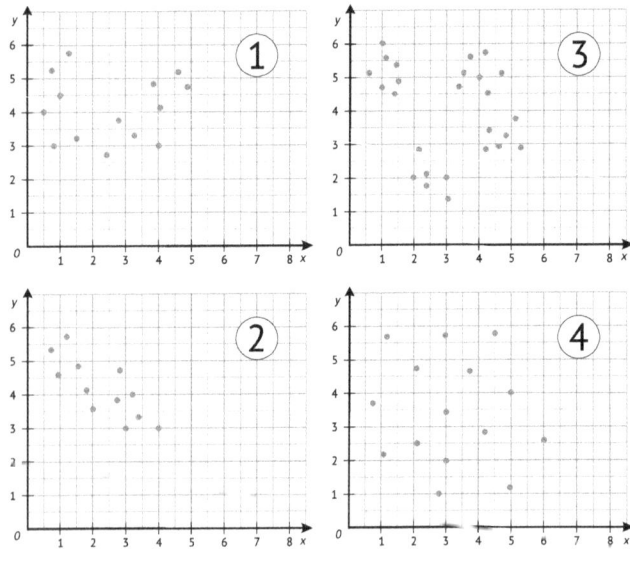

DAY 6
Challenge question

The change in the population of the Earth is shown in the chart below. Is this a linear association? _____

Year	1800	1927	1960	1974	1987	1999	2011
People, billion	1	2	3	4	5	6	7

8.G.C.9

112

WEEK 18

In this week, you will practice finding the best fit of a line on a given graph. You should understand that straight lines are used to model a potential relationship between two quantitative variables.

You can find detailed video explanations of each problem in the book by visiting: ArgoPrep.com/ccm8

WEEK 18 : DAY 1

1. Which line best fits the data on the graph?

   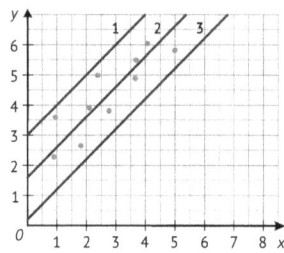

   A. 1
   B. 2
   C. 3
   D. None of the above.

2. Which of the rules should be used when drawing the line that best fits the data?

   A. The line should have a positive slope.
   B. The line should have a negative slope.
   C. The line should be horizontal.
   D. It is necessary to take into account the location of points on the scatter plot and the distance between them.

3. Draw a line that best fits the represented scatter plot.

   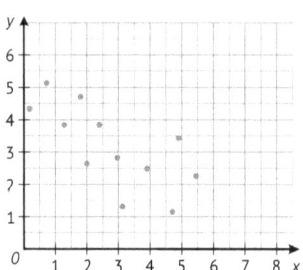

4. Which scatter plot shows an association that can be represented as a line?

   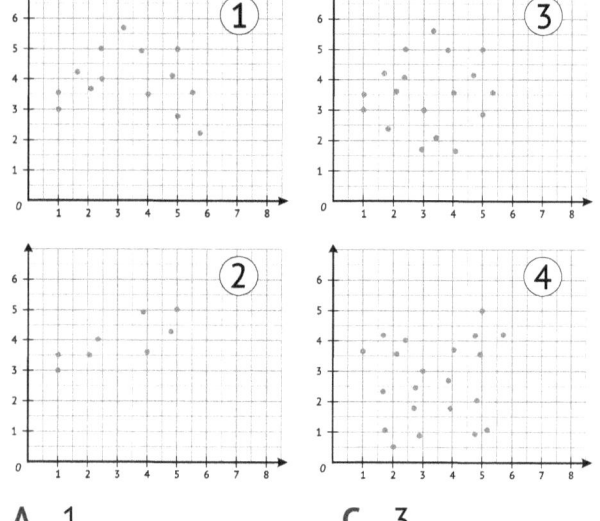

   A. 1
   B. 2
   C. 3
   D. 4

5. Draw a line that best fits the represented scatter plot.

   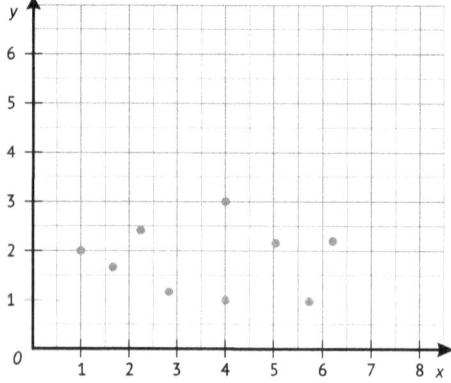

Scatter plots are useful to show how two variables are correlated.

WEEK 18 : DAY 2

1. Can a line of best fit be used to estimate the association between two quantitative variables?

   A. Yes, the line best estimates an association between two quantitative variables.
   B. No, the line does NOT allow you to estimate an association between two quantitative variables.
   C. Yes, only if the dots on the scatter plot are closely located on the line.
   D. It is not sufficient to draw one line to estimate an association between two quantitative variables.

   8.SP.A.2

2. Which statement is true?

   A. The line of best fit can determine the association of a scatter plot only when all dots are located on the line.
   B. The line of best fit can determine the association of a scatter plot if the correlation between the data is high.
   C. The line of best fit can determine the association of a scatter plot if the correlation between the data is very low.
   D. The line of best fit can determine any association of a scatter plot.

   8.SP.A.2

3. Which line best fits the data on the graph?

   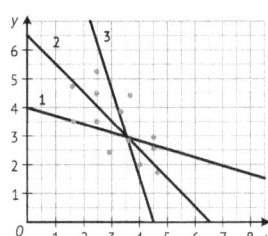

   A. 1
   B. 2
   C. 3
   D. None of the above.

   8.SP.A.2

4. Draw a line that best fits the represented scatter plot.

   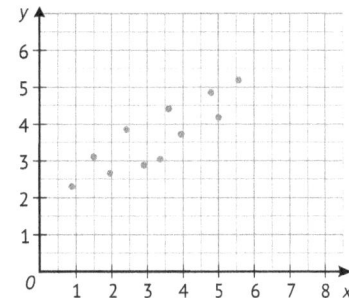

   8.SP.A.2

5. Draw a line that best fits the represented scatter plot.

   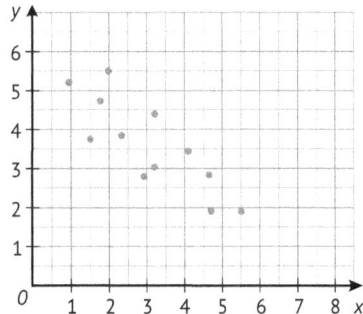

   8.SP.A.2

TIP of the DAY

A line of best fit is a straight line that best represents the data on a scatter plot.

115

WEEK 18 : DAY 3

1. Which line best fits the data on the graph?

   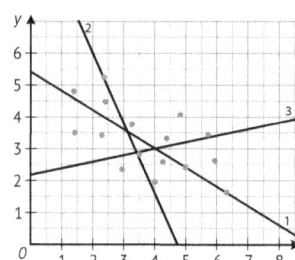

   A. 1
   B. 2
   C. 3
   D. None of the above.

   8.SP.A.2

2. Draw a line that best fits the represented scatter plot.

   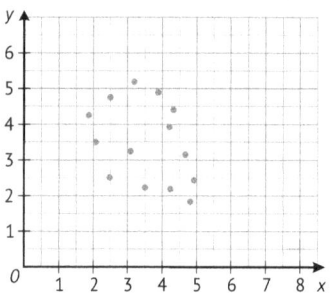

   8.SP.A.2

3. If the line of best fit shows an association between the data on the scatter plot, that means...

   A. Correlation between the data is weak.
   B. There is no association between the data.
   C. Variables are changing in one direction.
   D. Correlation between the data is strong.

   8.SP.A.2

4. Which statement about the data on the scatter plot below is true?

   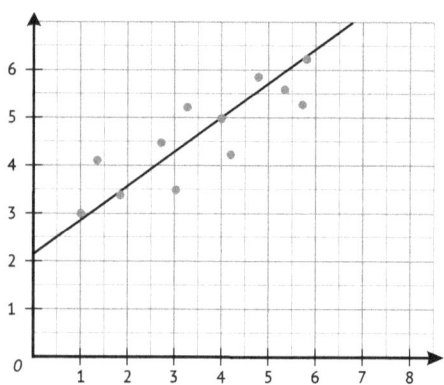

   A. Correlation between the data is strong.
   B. There is a negative association between the data.
   C. There is no correlation between the data.
   D. None of the above.

   8.SP.A.2

5. Is it possible to consider an association between the data as a linear one, if there is an outlier on the scatter plot?

   A. No, it is not.
   B. Yes, it is.
   C. Yes, only if all other data points have a close location to the line.
   D. It is impossible.

   8.SP.A.2

TIP of the DAY

We have talked a lot about correlation this week. Have you heard of the correlation coefficient? The correlation coefficient, usually labeled as r, has a value between -1.0 and 1.0. If r is 1.0, you have a perfect positive correlation. You will learn more about this in high school!

116

WEEK 18 : DAY 4

1. Find the line which best fits the data on the graph.

   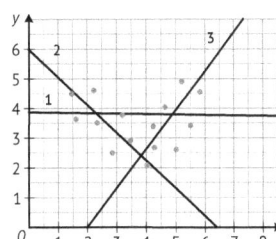

   A. 1
   B. 2
   C. 3
   D. None of the above.

2. How can the best fit line drawn on the scatter plot be useful?

   A. The line allows us to determine if a type of association between the data exists.
   B. The line allows us to determine the trend of changing variables on the scatter plot.
   C. The line allows us to assess how strong the correlation is between the data.
   D. All of the above above.

   8.SP.A.2

3. Draw a line that best fits the represented scatter plot.

   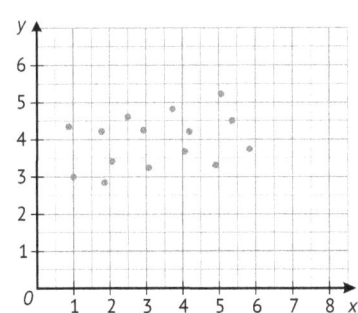

   8.SP.A.2

4. How many lines of best fit can be drawn in the scatter plot below to show the association between the two quantitative variables?

   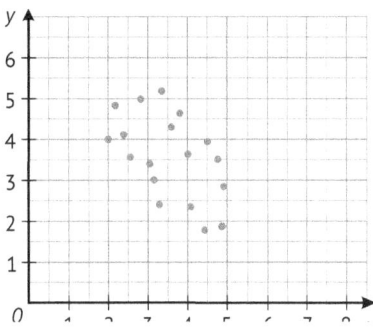

   A. One
   B. Two
   C. The line does not correspond to the association.
   D. There is no correct answer.

   8.SP.A.2

5. Draw a line which best fits the represented scatter plot.

   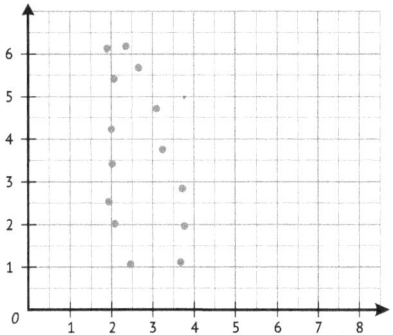

   8.SP.A.2

When scatter plots have no correlation, you cannot draw a line of best fit.

117

WEEK 18 : DAY 5

ASSESSMENT

1. Find the line which best fits the data on the graph.

   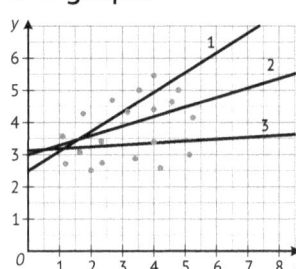

   A. 1
   B. 2
   C. 3
   D. None of the above.

   8.SP.A.2

2. What does it mean if all points of the scatter plot are on the best fit line?

   A. There is no correlation between the data.
   B. Correlation between the data is very strong.
   C. Correlation between the data is very weak.
   D. No conclusion can be drawn.

   8.SP.A.2

3. Draw a line which best fits the represented scatter plot.

   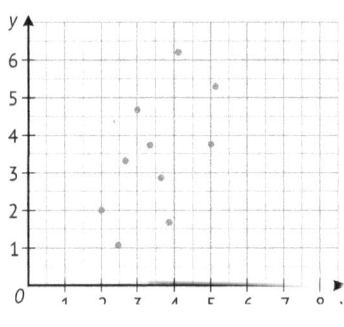

   8.SP.A.2

4. Which picture below shows a positive correlation between the two quantitative variables?

   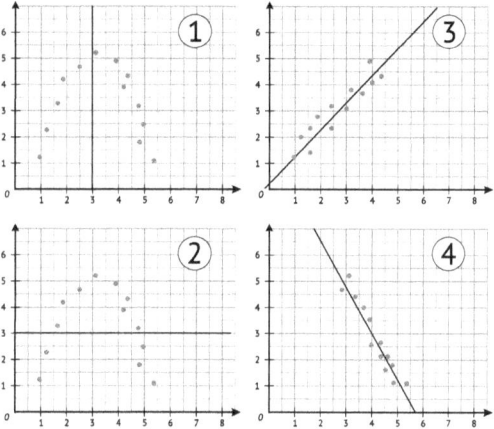

   A. 1   B. 2   C. 3   D. 4

   8.SP.A.2

5. Which of the following examples show a positive correlation?

   A. The more you eat, the less hungry you get.
   B. The older you get, the less energy you have.
   C. The heavier your car is, the fewer miles per gallon you will get.
   D. The longer you run, the more calories you will burn.

   8.SP.A.2

DAY 6
Challenge question

A student who has an increased number of absences has a decrease in grade point average. Is this an example of positive, negative or no correlation?

_____

8.SP.A.2

WEEK 19

Week 19 is all about working with the equation of a linear model and interpreting the slope and intercept.

You can find detailed video explanations of each problem in the book by visiting: ArgoPrep.com/ccm8

WEEK 19 : DAY 1

1. What is the equation of the line that best fits the data on the scatter plot?

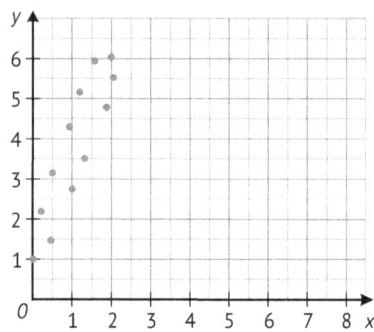

   A. $y = 2.5x$
   B. $y = 1 + 2.5x$
   C. $y = 2.5x - 1$
   D. $y = 1 - 2.5x$

Sweet Country Inc. makes sweets of different sizes. They found out that each additional cubic centimeter of the volume increases the weight of a product by 40 grams. **Using this data, solve questions 2-5.**

2. Which of the following linear equations describes the best fitted line for the data given above?

   A. $y = 20x$
   B. $y = 40x$
   C. $y = 0.4x$
   D. $y = 3x$

3. What is the slope of the line of best fit?

   A. 40
   B. 4
   C. 8
   D. $\frac{1}{4}$

4. What is the approximate weight of a confectionery product with a volume of 6 cm³?

   A. 240 g.
   B. 360 g.
   C. 40 g.
   D. 4 g.

5. What is the approximate volume of a confectionery product that has a weight of 300 g.?

   A. 7 cm³
   B. 7.5 cm³
   C. 8 cm³
   D. 8.2 cm³

6. The equation $y = 62 + 0.4x$ describes the association between the average daily air temperature (degrees F) and days of the month. What was the average daily temperature on the first day of the month?

   Answer: _____

TIP of the DAY

If you are given an equation of a line in the form $y = mx + b$, you can easily find the slope by looking at the value of m.

WEEK 19 : DAY 2

1. What is the equation of the line that best fits the data on the scatter plot?

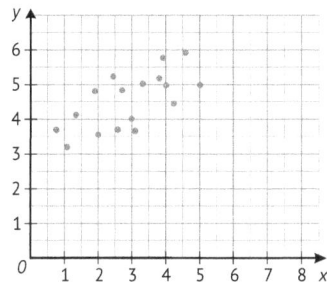

   A. $y = 0.5 + 3x$
   B. $y = 2.5 + 2x$
   C. $y = x + 3$
   D. $y = 0.5x + 3$

   8.SP.A.3

2. Which of the following linear equations best fits the model shown?

   A. $y = 8x$
   B. $y = 8 + 0.8x$
   C. $y = 0.8x$
   D. $y = 8 - 0.8x$

   8.SP.A.3

3. Which is the slope of the best fitted line?

   A. -8
   B. 10
   C. -0.8
   D. $\dfrac{10}{8}$

   8.SP.A.3

The school researched the number of additional hours (X) spent on solving problems and the number of mistakes (Y) made on exams. **Using the results below, answer questions 2-4.**

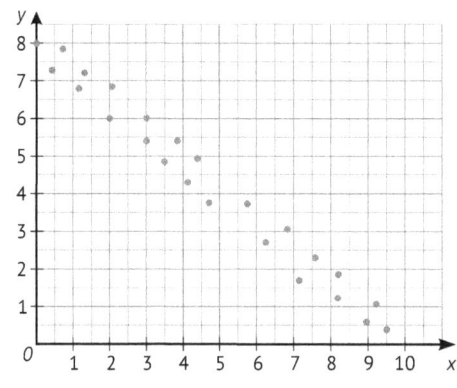

4. How many mistakes will a student approximately make in an exam if he practiced an additional 5 hours?

   A. 3
   B. 4
   C. 5
   D. 6

   8.SP.A.3

5. The equation $y = 62 + 0.4x$ describes the association between the average daily air temperature (degrees F) and days of the month. What was the average daily temperature on the fifteenth day of the month?

   Answer: _____

   8.SP.A.3

TIP of the DAY

If you are given an equation of a line in the form $y = mx + b$, you can easily find the y intercept by looking at the value of b.

WEEK 19 : DAY 3

1. What is the equation of the line that best fits the data on the scatter plot?

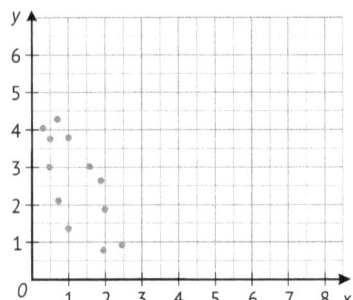

   A. $y = x - 5$
   B. $y = 5 + 2x$
   C. $y = 5 - 2x$
   D. $y = 2x - 5$

   8.SP.A.3

Mr. Bates' restaurant generates income of $2,000 per day. Each additional table approximately generates income of $200 per day. **Using the data provided, solve questions 2-6.**

2. Which of the following linear equations describes the best fit line for the data?

   A. $y = (2{,}000 + 200)x$
   B. $y = 200x$
   C. $y = 2{,}000 + 200x$
   D. $y = 200x - 2{,}000$

   8.SP.A.3

3. What is the slope of the best fit line?

   A. 1   C. 2,000
   B. 200   D. 2

   8.SP.A.3

4. What is the y-intercept of the best fitted line?

   A. 2,000   C. 2
   B. 200   D. 1

   8.SP.A.3

5. What will be the approximate income per day if Mr. Bates installs 5 additional tables?

   A. $1,000   C. $3,000
   B. $2,000   D. $4,000

   8.SP.A.3

6. Which of the following is true for the best fit line in this scenario?

   A. To increase income he needs to decrease the number of tables.
   B. Each additional table will double his income.
   C. Each additional table will probably increase income by $200.
   D. The number of tables negatively affects the income.

   8.SP.A.3

TIP of the DAY

If you are given a line on a graph and asked to find the equation of the line, you will always need to calculate the slope and also determine the y-intercept.

122

WEEK 19 : DAY 4

1. What is the equation of the line that best fits the data on the scatter plot?

   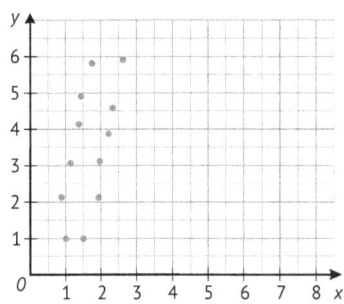

   A. $y = 5x - 5$
   B. $y = -5 - x$
   C. $y = 5 + 5x$
   D. $y = 5 - 5x$

A certain rabbit weighed 300 grams when it was gifted to Stephen. Every day the rabbit gained about 2 grams in weight. **Using this data, solve questions 2 - 5.**

2. Which linear equation best describes this data?

   A. $y = 2 + 300x$
   B. $y = 300 + 2x$
   C. $y = 2x - 300$
   D. $y = 300 - 2x$

3. What is the slope of the best fit line?

   A. 2
   B. 300
   C. 200
   D. 3

4. What does the *y*-intercept tell us when we draw a best fitted line?

   A. The minimum weight of the rabbit is 300 g.
   B. The rabbit weighed 300 g. when it was gifted to Stephen.
   C. The weight of the rabbit will increase to 300 g.
   D. The weight of the rabbit fluctuates.

5. How much will the rabbit weigh in 15 days?

   A. 315 g.
   B. 320 g.
   C. 330 g.
   D. 360 g.

When drawing a line of best fit, you want the line as close as possible to all the points.

WEEK 19 : DAY 5

ASSESSMENT

1. What is the equation of the line that best fits the data on the scatter plot?

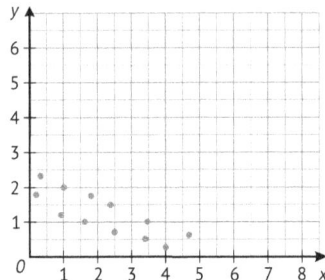

A. $y = \frac{1}{2}x + 2$

B. $y = 2 - 5x$

C. $y = 2 - \frac{2}{5}x$

D. $y = 2x - 5$

8.SP.A.3

The scatter plot and the regression line given below show the change in the population of the USA (in millions) by years. **Using the data, solve questions 2-4.**

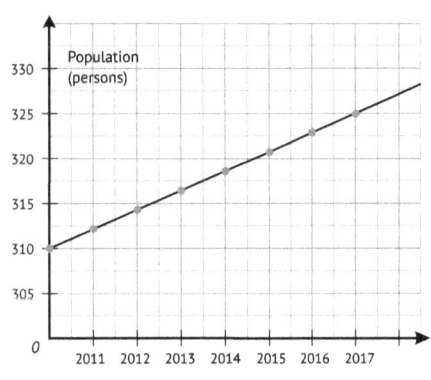

2. The line of best fit has a slope of 2.14. What is the best interpretation of this slope?

A. From 2010 to 2017, the US population increased by approximately 2.14 million people.
B. Every year the US population increases by approximately 2.14 million people.
C. The US population had approximately 2.14 million people in 2010.
D. Every year the US population increases by 2.14 times.

8.SP.A.3

3. What was the approximate population in the USA in 2014?

A. 316.28 million people
B. 318.59 million people
C. 319.75 million people
D. 320.9 million people

8.SP.A.3

4. What is the approximate number of population expected in the USA in 2019?

A. 326.12 million people
B. 327.5 million people
C. 330.14 million people
D. 332.4 million people

8.SP.A.3

DAY 6
Challenge question

Every hour of work decreases employees' productivity by approximately 2%. Write down the linear equation describing an association between the employees' productivity and the duration of their working day.

_____

8.SP.A.3

Week 20 is all about how to read and interpret two-way tables that summarize data between two variables.

You can find detailed video explanations of each problem in the book by visiting:
ArgoPrep.com/ccm8

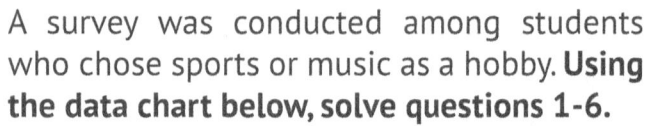

WEEK 20 : DAY 1

A survey was conducted among students who chose sports or music as a hobby. **Using the data chart below, solve questions 1-6.**

	boys	girls
sports	35	29
music	14	22

1. Which statement is true?

    A. More students chose sports as a hobby than music.
    B. More students chose music as a hobby than sports.
    C. The girls prefer playing music more than sports.
    D. The boys prefer playing music more than sports.

    8.SP.A.4

2. How many students chose music as their hobby?

    A. 64
    B. 49
    C. 36
    D. 51

    8.SP.A.4

3. How many girls have hobbies?

    A. 64   C. 36
    B. 49   D. 51

    8.SP.A.4

4. Which statement is FALSE?

    A. The boys who have a hobby prefer sports to music.
    B. The girls who have a hobby prefer sports to music.
    C. Any student who chose sports as their hobby is a boy.
    D. There are more girls with a selected hobby than boys according to the chart.

    8.SP.A.4

5. What percent of students chose sports as a hobby?

    Answer: _____

    8.SP.A.4

6. What percent of students who have a hobby are boys?

    Answer: _____

    8.SP.A.4

When calculating percents, be sure to remember the basic formula part / whole.

WEEK 20 : DAY 2

Students who study foreign languages were interviewed on what type of flower they like more: roses or tulips. **Using the results recorded below, solve the questions 1-6.**

	Those who study Spanish	Those who study French
Those who love roses	27	20
Those who love tulips	14	21
Those who have no preferences to any of these flowers	5	4

1. Which statement is true?

   A. There are more students studying French than those who study Spanish.
   B. More students who study Spanish prefer tulips.
   C. 51.6% of the respondents prefer roses.
   D. Most respondents have no preferences to any of these flowers.

   8.SP.A.4

2. How many interviewed students prefer tulips?

   A. 47   C. 46
   B. 35   D. 45

   8.SP.A.4

3. Which statement is FALSE?

   A. The students studying Spanish prefer roses.
   B. If a person prefers roses, then he/she studies Spanish.
   C. Twenty students who study French love roses.
   D. Students prefer roses more than tulips according to the chart above.

   8.SP.A.4

4. How many students study French?

   A. 41   C. 46
   B. 47   D. 45

   8.SP.A.4

5. What percent of the interviewed students don't have preferences to any of these flowers?

   A. 9.0%   C. 10.0%
   B. 9.9%   D. 10.1%

   8.SP.A.4

6. How many more students prefer roses than those who prefer tulips?

   Answer: _____

   8.SP.A.4

TIP of the DAY

A two-way data chart contains important information. Always be sure to read the title and headers so you know exactly what the data relates to.

WEEK 20 : DAY 3

Scientists conducted a survey on the topic: "How do people feel in a crowd?" among the residents of cities and towns. **Using the results given in two-way chart, solve questions 1-6.**

	The residents of the cities	The residents of the towns
Feel comfortable	42%	6%
Feel uncomfortable	8%	44%

1. Which statement is true?

   A. More people live in cities.
   B. More people live in towns.
   C. There are more people in cities than in towns.
   D. There are more people who feel comfortable in crowds among the residents of the cities.

2. If 1,200 people were interviewed, how many of them live in towns?

   A. 500
   B. 600
   C. 520
   D. 480

3. Which statement is FALSE?

   A. Most people live where they feel comfortable according to the data in the chart.
   B. Some residents live where they feel uncomfortable.
   C. A person is a resident of a town if he/she feels uncomfortable in a crowd.
   D. Most of the interviewed residents of cities feel comfortable in crowds.

4. If 1,200 people were interviewed, how many feel comfortable in crowds?

   A. 576   C. 600
   B. 587   D. 626

5. What percentage of respondents feel uncomfortable in crowds?

   A. 48%   C. 52%
   B. 50%   D. 54%

6. What percentage of city residents feel uncomfortable in crowds?

   A. 15%   C. 17%
   B. 16%   D. 18%

*When you see words like "**FALSE**" or "**MUST NOT BE TRUE**", try underlining them so you don't make any careless mistakes.*

WEEK 20 : DAY 4

Matthew interviewed his classmates and school teachers about whether they spend their weekends at home or outdoors. Matthew wrote down the results of his survey in the two-way chart. **Using the data from the chart, solve questions 1-6.**

	Classmates	Teachers
Like weekends at home	6	14
Like weekends outdoors	16	12

1. How many individuals did Matthew survey in total?

   A. 20
   B. 26
   C. 28
   D. 48

2. Which statement is true according to the chart above?

   A. From the surveyed respondents, more individuals prefer to spend their weekends at home.
   B. Most of Matthew's respondents are classmates.
   C. Most of Matthew's respondents are teachers.
   D. More adults like to spend their weekends outdoors.

3. Which statement is FALSE?

   A. More teachers like to spend their weekends at home than the outdoors.
   B. Teachers do like to spend their weekends outdoors.
   C. The classmates prefer to spend their weekends outdoors.
   D. Most of Matthew's respondents are teachers.

4. Determine the percentage of Matthew's respondents who prefer to spend their weekends outdoors?

   A. 58.3%
   B. 28.0%
   C. 48.0%
   D. 52.4%

5. What percent of Matthew's respondents are classmates?

   A. 22%
   B. 28%
   C. 45.8%
   D. 50.0%

6. How many more individuals prefer to spend their weekends outdoors than at home?

   Answer: _____

Do you know the difference between causation and correlation? Causation is when one event is the result of the other (think cause and effect). A correlation on the other hand is usually a statistical measure that we can express as a number that describes the direction of a relationship between two variables.

WEEK 20 : DAY 5

ASSESSMENT

The two-way chart below shows the data about the filling and the shape of the pies in a pastry shop. **Using the data from the chart, solve questions 1-6.**

	apples	blueberries
round	26	8
rectangular	16	21

1. Which statement is true?
    A. Most of the pies are round.
    B. Most of the pies have blueberry filling.
    C. More rectangular pies have blueberry filling than apple filling.
    D. Most of the rectangular pies have apple filling.

    8.SP.A.4

2. How many pies are there in the pastry shop in total?
    A. 34   C. 71
    B. 42   D. 84

    8.SP.A.4

3. Which statement is FALSE?
    A. There are more round pies with apple filling than with blueberry filling.
    B. There are more rectangular pies with blueberry filling than with apple filling.
    C. There are fewer round pies than rectangular pies.
    D. If a pie is round, then it has apple filling.

    8.SP.A.4

4. What percent of pies have apple filling?
    A. 42%   C. 61%
    B. 59.2%   D. 48.7%

    8.SP.A.4

5. What percent of pies are round with blueberry filling?
    A. 11.3%   C. 8.0%
    B. 12.4%   D. 9.6%

    8.SP.A.4

6. How many more pies are there with apple filling than with blueberry filling?

    Answer: _____

    8.SP.A.4

DAY 6
Challenge question

Define the word correlation in your own words. Give an example of a positive correlation.

_____
_____

8.SP.A.4

130

**Great job finishing all 20 weeks!
You should be ready for any test.**

ASSESSMENT

VIDEO EXPLANATIONS

ARGOPREP.COM

Try this assessment to see how much you've learned - good luck!

ASSESSMENT

1. Solve the linear equation $\frac{4}{5}x + 20 = \frac{5}{6}x$

   Answer: _____

   8.EE.C.7

2. Two lines are parallel. The first line was rotated 90°. Which statement is true?

   A. The rotated line is parallel to the second line.
   B. The rotated line is perpendicular to the second line.
   C. The rotated line is congruent to the second line.
   D. The rotated line does NOT cross the second line.

   8.G.A.1

3. Find the set which contains only rational numbers.

   A. $2\sqrt{3}, \frac{4}{5}, -4, 2.45$
   B. $2\sqrt{9}, 3\frac{6}{7}, -\sqrt{25}$
   C. $-16.0\overline{77}, 3.87234..., \sqrt{14}, \sqrt{144}$
   D. $\frac{17}{8}, -27.1, \frac{1}{\sqrt{36}}, \pi$

   8.NS.A.1

4. Which expression produces an irrational number?

   A. $2\sqrt{9} + \frac{1}{\sqrt{16}}$
   B. $7.0\overline{345} \times \frac{1}{2}$
   C. $\frac{\sqrt[3]{64}}{4}$
   D. $\frac{\sqrt[3]{36}}{3}$

   8.NS.A.1

5. What two integers are between $\sqrt{50}$?

   A. 5 and 6
   B. 6 and 7
   C. 7 and 8
   D. 8 and 9

   8.NS.A.2

6. Which expression is true?

   A. $4\sqrt{2} < 3\pi$
   B. $\sqrt{35} > 2\sqrt{10}$
   C. $\frac{1}{\sqrt{12}} > \frac{3}{\sqrt{18}}$
   D. $3\sqrt{26} < 2\sqrt{37}$

   8.NS.A.2

7. Place the numbers in order from least to greatest $2\sqrt{6}; -2\sqrt[3]{27}; -2\pi; 4\sqrt{2}$.

   Answer: _____

   8.NS.A.2

ASSESSMENT

8. Select the equivalent expression for $16x^{12}$.

    A. $(4x^2)^6$
    B. $(2^3x^6)^2$
    C. $(4x^6)^2$
    D. $4x^8 + x^4$

    8.EE.A.1

9. What is $\left(\dfrac{5x^{-2}}{8x^5}\right)^2$?

    A. $\dfrac{5x^{-4}}{8x^{10}}$
    B. $\dfrac{25}{64x^{14}}$
    C. $\dfrac{25x^{-4}}{8x^{10}}$
    D. $\dfrac{5}{8x^6}$

    8.EE.A.1

10. What is the solution of $\sqrt{144}$?

    Answer: _____

    8.EE.A.2

11. Which square root results in a rational number?

    A. $\sqrt{115}$
    B. $\sqrt{225}$
    C. $\sqrt{333}$
    D. $\sqrt{164}$

    8.EE.A.2

12. Find the quotient of the numbers $(6.8 \times 10^{12}) \div (1.7 \times 10^{-5})$.

    Answer: _____

    8.EE.A.3

13. What is 286 trillion expressed in scientific notation?

    A. 2.86×10^{12}
    B. 2.86×10^{13}
    C. 2.86×10^{14}
    D. 2.86×10^{15}

    8.EE.A.4

14. Which of the following lines has a slope -6?

    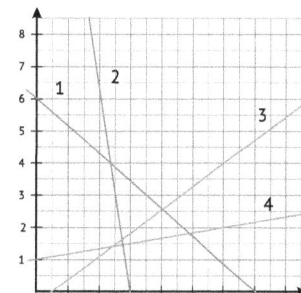

    A. 1
    B. 2
    C. 3
    D. 4

    8.EE.A.5

ASSESSMENT

15. What is the slope of the line $y = 25 - 7x$?

A. 25
B. 7
C. -25
D. -7

8.EE.B.6

16. Which point lies on the line $y = 2 + 4x$?

A. (5, 22)
B. (4, 16)
C. (12, 46)
D. (8, 33)

8.EE.B.6

17. Solve the linear equation $2x - 6 = 16 - 9x$.

A. 11
B. 22
C. 2
D. 6

8.EE.C.7

18. What is a solution to the equations $y - 9x - 15$ and $y - 18 - 2x$?

A. $x = 2$ and $y = 14$
B. $x = 3$ and $y = 15$
C. $x = 11$ and $y = 4$
D. $x = 3$ and $y = 12$

8.EE.C.8

19. Determine the coordinates of the common point for the two lines.

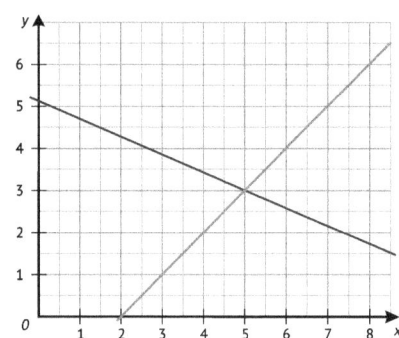

A. (3, 5)
B. (5, 3)
C. (2, 0)
D. (0, 5)

8.EE.C.8

20. Which set of points do NOT form a function?

A. (3, 4); (5, 8); (7, 12)
B. (6, 4); (6, 0); (6, 7)
C. (-2, 4); (0, 4); (2, 5)
D. (0, 7); (-2, 10); (4, -8)

8.F.A.1

21. Which of the following equations is NOT a function?

A. $y = 5x + 12$
B. $x - 4y = 49$
C. $34x = 12$
D. $2x^2 + 4y = 2x + 9$

8.F.A.1

ASSESSMENT

22. Which of the following functions is changing faster?

1

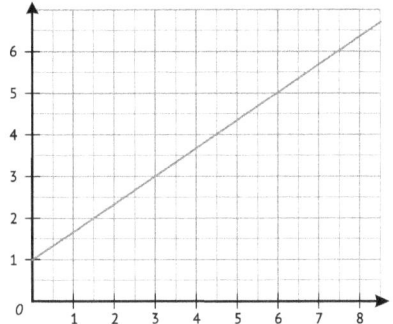

2

x	y
1	15
2	17
3	19
4	21
5	22

Answer: _____

8.F.A.2

23. What is the rate of change of a linear function that has the points (7, -2) and (9, 4)?

A. 2

B. $2\frac{1}{2}$

C. 3

D. $3\frac{1}{2}$

8.F.B.4

24. Which of the following expressions is a NONlinear function?

A. $34x = -2y$

B. $y = \frac{2-x}{x}$

C. $y = \frac{4+y}{2} + x$

D. $y = \frac{12+3x}{76}$

8.F.A.3

25. A linear function has the rate of change -3 and point (2, 9). What is the y-intercept of this function?

Answer: _____

8.F.B.4

26. Is the value of the function $y = 12x - 32$ decreasing or increasing, if the value of x is increasing?

Answer: _____

8.F.B.5

27. Which of the following functions is increasing constantly?

A. $y = -3x^2$

B. $y = 4 - 12x$

C. $y = 4x^2$

D. $y = -32 + 17x$

8.F.B.5

137

ASSESSMENT

28. How has the second shape changed from the initial one?

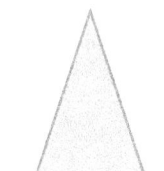

- A. Rotation
- B. Reflection
- C. Translation
- D. Dilation

8.G.A.1

29. Determine which two shapes are congruent?

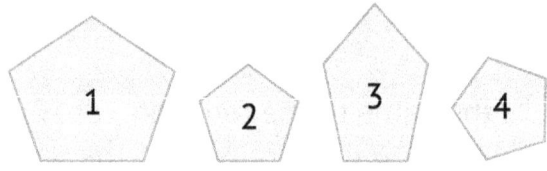

Answer: _____

8.G.A.2

30. The triangle with coordinates (-3, 5), (-2, 1), and (-1, 3) was reflected over the y axis. Find one coordinate from this new triangle.

- A. (-3, -5)
- B. (3, 5)
- C. (2, 4)
- D. (-1, -3)

8.G.A.3

31. Which of the following transformations will change the preimage into the image?

preimage   image

- A. Dilation
- B. Dilation and translation
- C. Dilation and Rotation
- D. Reflection

8.G.A.3

32. Can two squares be congruent if one has a side with the coordinates (3, 5) and (5, 1), and the second square has a side with the coordinates (-5, 2) and (-1, 4)? Explain your reasoning.

Answer: _____

8.G.A.4

33. The exterior angle of the triangle is 78°. What is the value of the conjugated interior angle?

Answer: _____

8.G.A.5

138

ASSESSMENT

34. Below are two parallel lines with the third line intersecting them. Which statement is true?

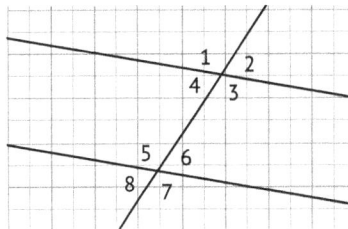

A. $m\angle 1 = m\angle 2$
B. $m\angle 2 = m\angle 4$
C. $m\angle 4 = m\angle 5$
D. $m\angle 5 = m\angle 2$

8.G.A.5

35. The triangle has sides that measure 9 cm, 12 cm and 15 cm. Is this a right triangle?

Answer: _____

8.G.B.6

36. The hypotenuse of the right triangle measures 26 cm in length and the leg measures 13 cm. What is the length of the other leg?

A. 12 cm
B. 13 cm
C. $13\sqrt{3}$ cm
D. $14\sqrt{4}$ cm

8.G.B.7

37. Find the diagonal of the square that has a perimeter of 20 cm.

A. 5 cm
B. $5\sqrt{2}$ cm
C. 6 cm
D. $6\sqrt{2}$ cm

8.G.B.7

38. The distance between point (6, 2) and another point is 15. What are the coordinates of the other point?

A. (9, 12)
B. (14, 10)
C. (16, 15)
D. (15, 14)

8.G.B.8

39. What are the coordinates of two points if the distance between them is 25?

A. (-3, 7) and (17, -8)
B. (5, 10) and (20, 24)
C. (8, -8) and (19, -12)
D. (-6, -3) and (13, 14)

8.G.B.8

40. Which of the following can be the coordinate points for a right triangle?

A. (6, 7), (15, 7), (8, 9)
B. (-3, 1), (-1, 1), (-3, 4)
C. (-8, 3), (2, -4), (0, 1)
D. (10, 12), (12, 16), (11, 23)

8.G.B.8

139

ASSESSMENT

41. Find the height of the cone if its volume is 486π cm³ and the radius is 9 cm.

   A. 15 cm
   B. 16 cm
   C. 17 cm
   D. 18 cm

   8.G.C.9

42. A cylindrical container for water has a radius of 4 feet and a height of 6 feet. It must be filled with $\frac{2}{3}$ of water. What is the volume of water that should be poured into the container?

   Answer: _____

   8.G.C.9

43. What would be an example of a negative association?

   A. The more items Mary orders at a restaurant, the higher her bill will be.
   B. The more hours you run, the less you weigh.
   C. The more hours Noah spends studying Math, the higher his GPA is.
   D. None of the above.

   8.SP.A.1

44. A coach collected data on how many hours students of different ages ran in a week. Data for 8 participants are shown below. Plot the data in a scatter plot.

Running (hours)	2	3	5	4	8	7	9	8
Age	8	9	10	11	12	13	14	15

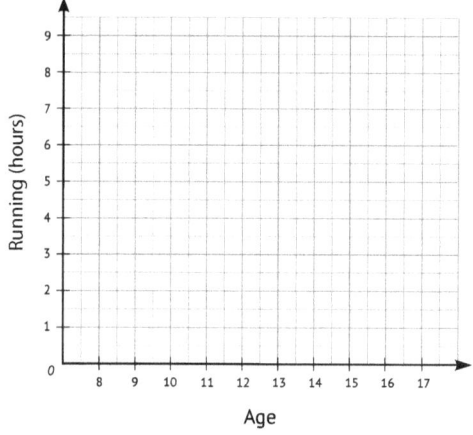

8.SP.A.1

45. Find the line which best fits the data on the graph.

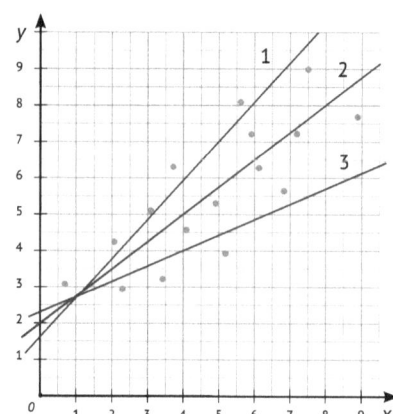

   A. 1
   B. 2
   C. 3
   D. None of these

   8.SP.A.2

140

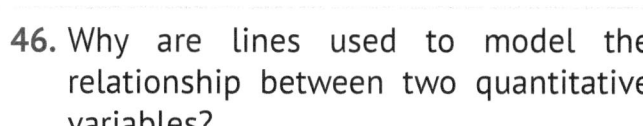

ASSESSMENT

46. Why are lines used to model the relationship between two quantitative variables?

   A. It can be drawn easily.
   B. A line shows a direction of change in the data.
   C. A line can be drawn through most dots of a scatter plot.
   D. The data often has a linear association between each other.

   8.SP.A.2

47. What is the equation of the best fitted line for the scatter plot shown below?

   A. $y = 1.75x + 7$
   B. $y = 7 - 2.5x$
   C. $y = -1.75x + 7$
   D. $y = 7 - 3x$

   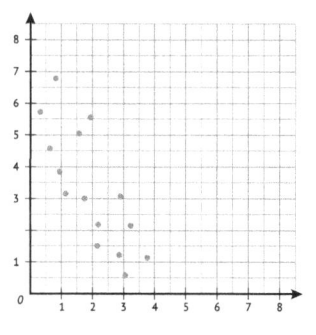

   8.SP.A.3

48. Each hour of exercising in the gym leads to a loss of 2 ounces of weight. Write a linear equation that best fits the association between hours of exercising and Mrs. Sanders' weight loss if she currently weighs 200 pounds.

   Answer: _____

   8.SP.A.3

The two-way chart below shows the data about the filling of pastries in a pastry shop. **Using the data from the chart, solve questions 49 - 50.**

	Chocolate	Vanilla
Éclair	35	14
Muffin	24	24

49. Which statement is true?

   A. Most of the muffins have chocolate filling.
   B. Most of the muffins have vanilla filling.
   C. Most of the éclairs have vanilla filling.
   D. There are more éclairs than muffins.

   8.SP.A.4

50. What percent of éclairs have vanilla filling?

   A. 28.6%
   B. 30.2%
   C. 25.8%
   D. 40.6%

   8.SP.A.4

141

ANSWER KEY

WEEK 1

DAY 1
1. B
2. A
3. D
4. B
5. rational
6. 0.8; yes

DAY 2
1. A
2. C
3. A
4. B
5. $\frac{3}{8}$; rational
6. rational

DAY 3
1. C
2. B
3. $\frac{8}{9}$
4. B
5. irrational
6. C

DAY 4
1. B
2. C
3. irrational
4. Answers may vary
5. B
6. C

DAY 5
1. D
2. B
3. A
4. B
5. rational
6. B

WEEK 2

DAY 1
1. C
2. D
3. A
4. B
5. $\frac{\sqrt{68}}{2}$; $5\sqrt{17}$; $4\sqrt{32}$; 26
6. 8

DAY 2
1. B
2. A
3. C
4. D
5. (number line with $\sqrt{44}$ marked between 6 and 7)
6. $2\sqrt{32}$; $9\frac{25}{40}$; $\sqrt{74}$; $\frac{\sqrt{85}}{3}$

DAY 3
1. B
2. D
3. $9\frac{6}{7}$
4. D
5. See picture 1
6. B

DAY 4
1. $\sqrt{21}$ — m, -2π — n, $-2\sqrt{14}$ — k, $\sqrt{5}$ — s
2. B
3. D
4. B
5. $7\sqrt{28} > 6\sqrt{30}$
6. A

DAY 5
1. B
2. C
3. $8 < \sqrt{67} < 9$
4. See picture 2
5. B
6. C

WEEK 3

DAY 1
1. B
2. D
3. C
4. $16x^{14}$
5. A
6. 6

DAY 2
1. D
2. C
3. B
4. A
5. $2x^{-2}$
6. $12x^3$

DAY 3
1. B
2. C
3. B
4. A
5. $\left(\frac{2x^4}{y^5}\right)^2$
6. $k = 7$; $n = -10$

DAY 4
1. C
2. D
3. B
4. $2x^{30}$
5. A
6. -2

DAY 5
1. D
2. B
3. C
4. $\frac{2}{x^7}$
5. A
6. $x = 4$

WEEK 4

DAY 1
1. B
2. C
3. A
4. B
5. A
6. 6

DAY 2
1. A
2. B
3. C
4. A
5. B
6. 5

DAY 3
1. C
2. D
3. D
4. C
5. C
6. 4×10^6

DAY 4
1. D
2. B
3. B
4. D
5. 2×10^{10}
6. 5×10^2

DAY 5
1. A
2. D
3. B
4. C
5. Mass of Jupiter is 317 times greater than mass of Earth
6. approximately 10 times

144

ANSWER KEY

WEEK 5

DAY 1
1. D
2. B
3. D
4. 1.618×10^5 sq km
5. 0.000003785
6. A

DAY 2
1. A
2. C
3. B
4. C
5. 2.9×10^4 ft
6. 1.03×10^{-3} kilo/cm^3

DAY 3
1. B
2. B
3. 1.66×10^{-27} kilo
4. C
5. The slope is 3.5

DAY 4
1. A
2. B
3. C
4. 1.5
5. 1.2 times

DAY 5
1. B
2. D
3. C
4. See picture 3
5. C
6. C

WEEK 6

DAY 1
1. B
2. A
3. D
4. C
5. 8
6. $y = x + 4$

DAY 2
1. C
2. D
3. B
4. C
5. -5
6. 3

DAY 3
1. C
2. $y = -3x + 6$
3. D
4. A
5. $y = 6$
6. B

DAY 4
1. A
2. C
3. D
4. A
5. The equation has an unending quantity of solutions
6. $x = 1.5$

DAY 5
1. D
2. B
3. D
4. D
5. B
6. The equation does not have a solution

WEEK 7

DAY 1
1. B
2. C
3. C
4. B
5. There is no intersection point.
6. $x = -2; y = -11$

DAY 2
1. A
2. C
3. A
4. A
5. C

DAY 3
1. D
2. B
3. D
4. A
5. 48 cups of latte and 24 cups of cappuccino

DAY 4
1. C
2. B
3. 18 steaks and 6 burgers
4. B
5. 7 bales of 100 pounds and 8 bales of 150 pounds

DAY 5
1. D
2. B
3. 4 T-shirts and 2 shorts
4. D
5. 20 hens and 10 goats
6. B

WEEK 8

DAY 1
1. A
2. B
3. D
4. If the value of x is increasing, the value of y is decreasing.
5. 2

DAY 2
1. A
2. C
3. B
4. A
5. yes

DAY 3
1. -1
2. C
3. B
4. C
5. The value of y will change from 44 to 24

DAY 4
1. 0.5 or 3.5
2. A
3. Specimen A
4. A
5. A

DAY 5
1. D
2. It will change from 8 to -4
3. C
4. 140
5. 1,900

ANSWER KEY

WEEK 9

DAY 1
1. B
2. A
3. D
4. A
5. 6
6. A. 2
   B. 5

DAY 2
1. A
2. B
3. B
4. C
5. See picture 4
6. the slope is -16, initial value is - 25.

DAY 3
1. C
2. C
3. A
4. A
5. $-\dfrac{1}{4}$
6. -10

DAY 4
1. C
2. D
3. D
4. C
5. A. 5
   B. 100

DAY 5
1. B
2. C
3. D
4. B
5. the slope is 1, the initial value is -30.
6. C

WEEK 10

DAY 1
1. A
2. B
3. B
4. B
5. The value of the function is decreasing.

DAY 2
1. D
2. B
3. C
4. A
5. 1

DAY 3
1. A
2. D
3. D
4. D
5. 3

DAY 4
1. C
2. A
3. 4
4. B
5. B
6. The value of the function is increasing.

DAY 5
1. B
2. A
3. 2
4. D
5. Yes, it does.
6. D

WEEK 11

DAY 1
1. C
2. D
3. B
4. A
5. None
6. None

DAY 2
1. A
2. A
3. B
4. D
5. They will stay parallel.
6. reflection

DAY 3
1. D
2. D
3. C
4. C
5. 180°
6. reflection

DAY 4
1. B
2. A
3. No. Rotation does NOT change the measure of an angle.
4. D
5. 1 and 3
6. C

DAY 5
1. A
2. They are not congruent.
3. B
4. D
5. A
6. C

WEEK 12

DAY 1
1. D
2. D
3. B
4. B
5. They are congruent.

DAY 2
1. B
2. C
3. B
4. D
5. reflection and rotation

DAY 3
1. B
2. C
3. B
4. B
5. (-2,-1), (-1, 3), (2, 4), (4, 1)
6. (6, 20) and (12, 8)

DAY 4
1. D
2. D
3. (-4, 4), (4, 4), (4, -4), (-4, -4)
4. C
5. C

DAY 5
1. C
2. Answers may vary
3. C
4. No, they can not.
5. 6 units

146

ANSWER KEY

WEEK 13

DAY 1	DAY 2	DAY 3	DAY 4	DAY 5
1. D	1. A	1. B	1. B	1. C
2. C	2. C	2. A	2. C	2. D
3. A	3. B	3. C	3. A	3. No, it isn't.
4. D	4. D	4. B	4. Yes, it is.	4. B
5. For the right triangles	5. 95°	5. the Pythagorean Theorem	5. C	5. They are similar.
6. 120°	6. Yes, it is. But if only they are right.	6. It is a right isosceles triangle		6. 360°

WEEK 14

DAY 1	DAY 2	DAY 3	DAY 4	DAY 5
1. A	1. B	1. D	1. B	1. B
2. B	2. C	2. C	2. A	2. C
3. B	3. B	3. C	3. A	3. D
4. B	4. D	4. D	4. A	4. C
5. 12 cm	5. No, it won't. A frame is smaller than the picture.	5. 150 meters	5. $16 \times \sqrt{7}$ yd	5. No, she can not.
6. $7 \times \sqrt{5}$	6. 10 ft	6. $4 \times \sqrt{34}$ cm	6. $\sqrt{277}$ km	6. 15 km

WEEK 15

DAY 1	DAY 2	DAY 3	DAY 4	DAY 5
1. B	1. C	1. A	1. D	1. B
2. A	2. A	2. C	2. D	2. C
3. D	3. B	3. A	3. A	3. B
4. B	4. B	4. D	4. D	4. C
5. $\sqrt{50}$	5. 5	5. $\sqrt{26}$	5. $\sqrt{58}$	5. 17
6. 15	6. 91	6. $9\sqrt{2}$	6. $4\sqrt{2}$	6. 80

WEEK 16

DAY 1	DAY 2	DAY 3	DAY 4	DAY 5
1. B	1. A	1. D	1. D	1. D
2. B	2. C	2. A	2. B	2. B
3. A	3. B	3. D	3. A	3. C
4. C	4. C	4. D	4. A	4. C
5. Yes, it will.	5. The Morgans	5. 1,130.4 cm^3	5. 4 glasses	5. 38
6. 2	6. Yes, it will.	6. 20	6. 14,130 in^3	

ANSWER KEY

WEEK 17

DAY 1
1. B
2. B
3. See picture 5
4. B

DAY 2
1. C
2. B
3. C
4. B.

DAY 3
1. A
2. C
3. B
4. C
5. D
6. C

DAY 4
1. A
2. C
3. F
4. See picture 6
5. A

DAY 5
1. B
2. B
3. A
4. C
5. D

WEEK 18

DAY 1
1. B
2. D
3. See picture 7
4. B
5. See picture 8

DAY 2
1. C
2. B
3. B
4. See picture 9
5. See picture 10

DAY 3
1. A
2. See picture 11
3. D
4. A
5. C

DAY 4
1. D
2. D
3. See picture 12
4. A
5. See picture 13

DAY 5
1. B
2. B
3. See picture 14
4. C
5. D

WEEK 19

DAY 1
1. B
2. B
3. A
4. A
5. B
6. 62.4°F

DAY 2
1. D
2. D
3. C
4. B
5. 68°F

DAY 3
1. C
2. C
3. B
4. A
5. C
6. C

DAY 4
1. A
2. B
3. A
4. B
5. C

DAY 5
1. C
2. B
3. B
4. C

WEEK 20

DAY 1
1. A
2. C
3. D
4. C
5. 64%
6. 49%

DAY 2
1. C
2. B
3. B
4. D
5. B
6. 12

DAY 3
1. D
2. B
3. C
4. A
5. C
6. B

DAY 4
1. D
2. C
3. B
4. A
5. C
6. 8

DAY 5
1. C
2. C
3. D
4. B
5. A
6. 13

ANSWER KEY

Picture

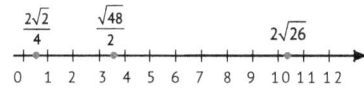

Picture 1

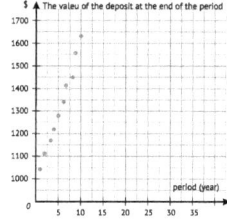

Picture 6

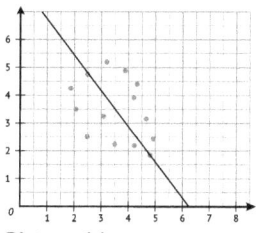

Picture 11

Picture 2

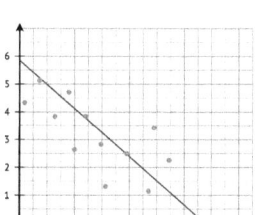

Picture 7

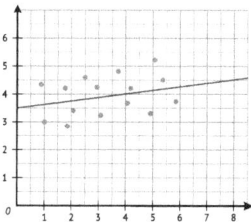

Picture 12

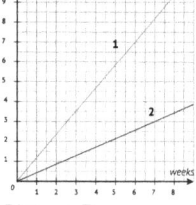

Picture 3

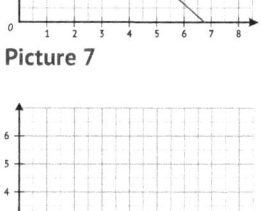

Picture 8

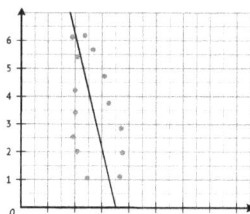

Picture 13

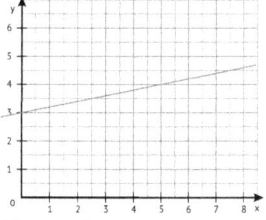

Picture 4

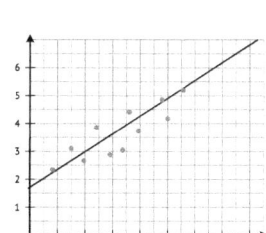

Picture 9

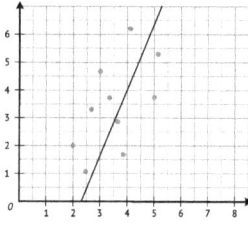

Picture 14

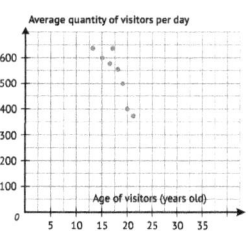

Picture 5

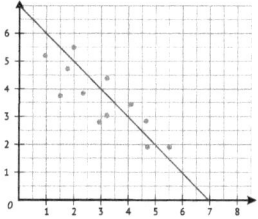

Picture 10

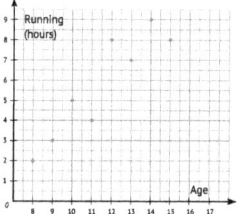

Picture 15

ANSWER KEY

Challenge Question

WEEK 1
rational number

WEEK 2
$\dfrac{5}{\sqrt{44}} > \dfrac{4}{\sqrt{35}}$

WEEK 3
$\dfrac{x^{-24}}{y^{-12}}$

WEEK 4
2

WEEK 5
3.8×10^9

WEEK 6
$\dfrac{\sqrt{6}}{3}$

WEEK 7
$x = 4.8; y = 3.4$

WEEK 8
$x = 5$

WEEK 9
-4

WEEK 10
It is changing its direction

WEEK 11
The lines are horizontal and parallel. The distance between them is 3 cm

WEEK 12
(3, -3), (6, -3), (6, -6)

WEEK 13
They are similar

WEEK 14
130 meters

WEEK 15
26

WEEK 16
sphere

WEEK 17
No, it isn't

WEEK 18
Negative correlation

WEEK 19
$y = 100 - 2x$

WEEK 20
Answers may vary

ANSWER KEY

Assessment

1. $x = 600$
2. B
3. B
4. D
5. C
6. A
7. $-2\pi, -2\sqrt[3]{27}, 2\sqrt{6}, 4\sqrt{2}$
8. C
9. B
10. 12 or -12
11. B
12. 4×10^{17}
13. C
14. B
15. D
16. A
17. C
18. D
19. B
20. B
21. C
22. 2
23. C
24. B
25. 15
26. The value of the function is increasing.
27. D
28. A
29. 2 and 4
30. B
31. C
32. yes
33. 102°
34. B
35. Yes, it is
36. C
37. B
38. D
39. A
40. B
41. D
42. 64π ft^3
43. B
44. See picture 15
45. B
46. D
47. C
48. $y = 200 - 0.125x$
49. D
50. A

You can scan this QR code to access *video explanations*.

KIDS WINTER ACADEMY

Kids Winter Academy by ArgoPrep covers material learned in September through December so your child can reinforce the concepts they should have learned in class. We recommend using this particular series during the winter break. These workbooks include two weeks of activities for math, reading, science, and social studies. Best of all, you can access detailed video explanations to all the questions on our website.

SOCIAL STUDIES

Social Studies Daily Practice Workbook by ArgoPrep allows students to build foundational skills and review concepts. Our workbooks explore social studies topics in depth with ArgoPrep's 5 E's to build social studies mastery.

www.ingramcontent.com/pod-product-compliance
Lightning Source LLC
Chambersburg PA
CBHW051804100526
44592CB00016B/2555